Cambridge Elements ≡

Elements in New Religious Movements
Series Editor
Rebecca Moore
San Diego State University
Founding Editor
†James R. Lewis
Wuhan University

NEW RELIGIOUS MOVEMENTS AND SCIENCE

Stefano Bigliardi
Al Akhawayn University in Ifrane

CAMBRIDGE
UNIVERSITY PRESS

Shaftesbury Road, Cambridge CB2 8EA, United Kingdom

One Liberty Plaza, 20th Floor, New York, NY 10006, USA

477 Williamstown Road, Port Melbourne, VIC 3207, Australia

314–321, 3rd Floor, Plot 3, Splendor Forum, Jasola District Centre,
New Delhi – 110025, India

103 Penang Road, #05–06/07, Visioncrest Commercial, Singapore 238467

Cambridge University Press is part of Cambridge University Press & Assessment,
a department of the University of Cambridge.

We share the University's mission to contribute to society through the pursuit of
education, learning and research at the highest international levels of excellence.

www.cambridge.org
Information on this title: www.cambridge.org/9781009108393

DOI: 10.1017/9781009104203

First published 2023

A catalogue record for this publication is available from the British Library.

ISBN 978-1-009-10839-3 Paperback
ISSN 2635-232X (online)
ISSN 2635-2311 (print)

New Religious Movements and Science

Elements in New Religious Movements

DOI: 10.1017/9781009104203
First published online: April 2023

Stefano Bigliardi
Al Akhawayn University in Ifrane
Author for correspondence: Stefano Bigliardi, S.Bigliardi@aui.ma

Abstract: This Element shows how new religious movements (NRMs) variously conceptualize science and provides readers with an overview of the scholarly conversation surrounding this phenomenon. Section 1 describes five movements that, in different ways, include relevant references to science in their doctrines: Dianetics/Scientology, the Raëlian Movement, Falun Gong, Stella Azzurra (an Italian Santo Daime group), and Bambini di Satana (an Italian Satanist group). The conceptualization of science within these movements is examined in reference to official beliefs conveyed by the writings and claims of their respective leaders, but ethnographic work among affiliates is included as well. Section 2 reconstructs academic contributions by scholars who identify notable trends in the approaches to science within NRMs, or have developed typologies to describe that very understanding. Section 3 concludes the discussion of NRMs and science by offering suggestions regarding novel directions that the study of their relationship may take.

Keywords: new religious movements, religion and science, new religious movements and science, religion and pseudoscience, pseudoscience

ISBNs: 9781009108393 (PB), 9781009104203 (OC)
ISSNs: 2635-232X (online), 2635-2311 (print)

Contents

Introduction

This Element introduces its readers to the fact that new religious movements (henceforth NRMs) include varied and complex conceptualizations of science in their beliefs. It also introduces readers to scholars' conversations concerning this fact. Section 1 elaborates on five NRMs that, in different ways, include significant reference to science in their respective teachings. These movements are Scientology (which includes the doctrine and practice called Dianetics), the Raëlians, Falun Gong, Stella Azzurra (a Santo Daime group), and the Satanist organization Bambini di Satana.

Section 1 begins by presenting case studies to underscore that any NRM's conceptualization of science is invariably given, and should therefore be understood, within the context of its doctrines, including their modifications over time. As important as the discussion of science may be for a given NRM, extracting and extrapolating it from the NRM's worldview would be an oversimplification. Ultimately, the focus is here on NRMs' theology, not on theories developed by specialists in the philosophy of science that can be distilled without losing their gist. Arguably, members are drawn to a movement because of its ability as a whole to make sense of their existential experience. This Element aims to impart a deep understanding of the movements in question from the (academic) viewpoint of a nonmember. Arguably, there always will be a hiatus between a believer's self-perception (the emic perspective) and any scholarly reconstruction (the etic perspective), no matter how extensive and neutral. However, a good academic analysis should still strive for comprehensiveness. Therefore, a "bottom-up," holistic approach seemingly makes for a better starting point. That being said, I shall go back to the emic/etic distinction toward the end of the Element and problematize it.

The presentation of each case study is divided into two subsections. The first one narratively introduces the movement's history and beliefs, including its references to science, while the second one relies on scholarly literature (including my own) to analyze the movement's conceptualization of science and draw comparisons with the other movements discussed. I focus on NRMs' texts with emphasis on those of their respective founders. However, I do include references to, and reflection on, conceptualizations of science offered by NRM members detected through ethnographic work.

I have yet to define the term science. In a broad sense, science is any kind of structured knowledge, yet readers are likely to have intuitively associated the term with fields like biology, physics, or medicine – what one may call the natural sciences. There is a wide spectrum of interpretations of what, if anything, sets natural science apart from other fields. Briefly put, on one end of the spectrum one finds realist definitions according to which there is a reality out there independent of us, thus an objective description of the world is possible; empirical, mathematical, peer-checked methods allow us to approach a correct description of that "reality." On the other end of the spectrum, one finds constructivist approaches according to which natural science, as well as the very "reality" it refers to, is produced socially, not unlike other fields. In between, one finds a position like Thomas Kuhn's (1922–96), according to which scientists do concern themselves with reality, yet their selection of specific portions of reality, as well as of the very concepts and methods through which they study it, may be subject to peer pressures and subjective factors; however, Kuhn is inclined to believe that "object-ive reality" tends to prevail in the long run and that a "paradigm" of research may be superseded and annulled when evidence contrary to it becomes too large to ignore (Kuhn 1962). A detailed discussion of the myriad philosophical interpret-ations of science falls beyond the scope of this Element. I am nevertheless aware of the complexity and the challenges represented by such debates.

I began my research on NRMs also being aware that one should first capture what they claim before projecting any other vision on them. Therefore, I have opted for some stipulations. First, I offer here a study of science as the NRMs under examination discuss it, adopting what one may call a nominalist approach. In other words, I focus on NRMs in whose texts and teachings the terms "science" and "scientific" feature prominently: it is such usage that I primarily reconstruct. As we will see, the semantic spectrum covered by such terms as used in the different movements usually does include science meant as the study of the natural world, but it also surpasses it. Quite often, the discussion of science includes reference to technology as well: the practical application of science through artifacts that extend and enhance humans' knowledge of, and control over, the world.

I integrate this approach with a further stipulation, extending the analysis to the discussion of terms such as physics, biology, chemistry, and medicine, as well as of words and concepts that one would commonsensically associate with them, such as atom, cell, and healing.

In fact, even a nominalist and commonsense analysis inevitably carries within itself certain meanings and undertones. However, I am also convinced that the very bottom-up, general approach I adopt can mitigate my biases, thus providing the reader with a reasonable and respectful entry point into the belief systems discussed.

In the interest of transparency, I must add that, in other contexts, I rely on a realist concept of science to make prescriptive statements and draw critical assessments. In fact, in different publications I even have defined some NRM teachings as pseudoscientific. This may elicit irritation on behalf of colleagues in the social sciences who, with a few exceptions, strive to be as neutral as possible. Some contend that any criticism leveled at NRMs ends up fueling the ideological and practical persecutions that such movements may undergo. This is not my perspective. I also belong to a junior cohort of NRM scholars that is admittedly less directly involved in the cult wars of the twentieth century; that is, the often vehement debates over the role of NRM experts in regard to those very NRMs' social perceptions and institutional handling. Additionally, I regard NRM teachings as proposed models for the explanation of certain phenomena, as well as methods for the achievement of certain results that, as such, may well be respectfully scrutinized and evaluated in reference to criteria such as logical consistency and effectiveness. At the same time, I do see why other scholars may disagree, and strongly at that. Moreover, I am familiar with the challenge of coming up with a clear-cut and universal definition of pseudoscience (cf. Pigliucci & Boudry 2013).

That being said, all such discussions exceed the scope of this Element. To be sure, I do mention criticism leveled at the ways in which different NRMs conceptualize science, and I do resort to the term pseudoscientific in order to qualify them. This, however, is not done while offering my own perspective, but rather through referencing stances represented by various critics of NRMs. This discussion warrants reconstruction considering that the disapproval of certain NRMs, or of some of their beliefs, often crucially impacts the very way in which leaders and members of such NRMs perceive and present themselves.

Defining an NRM is challenging, too. Prominent scholars are divided over the criteria to adopt to define them, and advance different suggestions resulting from their respective backgrounds. For instance, religion historian J. G. Melton proposed that new religions, rather than sharing common attributes, are those that exist in a contested space because they are pushed to the fringes of culture by dominant voices in the religious culture and in the secular one (Melton 2004). Sociologist Eileen Barker emphasized the "newness" of NRMs in terms of beliefs, practices, organization, location, and membership; newness of membership, she underlined, is marked by special behavior, since converts tend to be more enthusiastic and vulnerable than members born into a religion. Additionally, NRMs are likely to undergo rapid and radical change, especially as a result of the founder's death. Barker recognized as well, however, that one religion's "newness" can be appreciated by way of comparison with other religions and is therefore a relative concept, and that the question "when does a new religion stop being new?" remains open (Barker 2004). Sociologist David G. Bromley defined new religious groups in reference to their alignment – in other words, NRMs' perceived low congruence with dominant culture and institutions results in constant disputes and negotiations, including over their very definition as religions. Bromley recognized, however, that movements thus described are placed on a spectrum (Bromley 2004). Independent scholar of the sociology of religion Thomas Robbins suggested distinguishing "new religions" and "alternative religions." The former are those that emerged recently as symbolically and organizationally independent, the latter are in tension with their sociocultural environment. While new religions can be alternative and vice versa, there is no perfect correlation between the two categories (Robbins 2004). For this Element I have adopted a pragmatic approach. On the one hand, I thought it reasonable to assume familiarity with NRMs and the debates surrounding their definition on behalf of my reader. On the other hand, I once again opted for a nominalist approach. One may say that NRMs ultimately are what NRM scholars study. The movements discussed here are widely recognized by the scholarly community, having been tackled in academic literature whose amount is, in some cases, staggering. Although Bambini di Satana appears to be an exception, Satanism, of which they are an expression, is widely explored by scholars.

Other factors make the selection of the NRMs discussed here significant. To begin with, while inevitably relying, and drawing, on scholarly literature, for each of them I conducted my own research on primary sources. Secondly, they represent NRMs' diversity in terms of geographical and cultural origin, diffusion, development, and structure. Dianetics and Scientology originated in the United States in the 1950s. The Church of Scientology is currently led by the founder's first successor, and it has spread globally, claiming its membership to be in the millions – while critics guess tens of thousands (Introvigne 2017). The Raëlian Movement originated in France in the early 1970s and, at the moment of writing, it is led by its founder. It has spread to other countries, including Canada (in particular, Québec), Japan (where the founder currently resides), and Burkina Faso. In a 2020 interview, Raëlian leader and spokesperson Dr. Brigitte Boisselier (more on her later), when asked about the movement's followers, replied, "we're probably reaching 100,000 now" (Shamir 2020). Falun Gong emerged in the early 1980s in China. Its founder left the country in 1996 and is currently a US permanent resident. Membership estimates in China vary between 2.1 and 2.3 million according to the Chinese government and 70–80 million according to the movement, to which one should add 20 million outside of China, again according to the movement (Penny 2012: 7). Stella Azzurra is an Italian branch of the Brazilian religion Santo Daime, whose diffusion is global yet contained, counting some 20,000 practitioners worldwide, 4,000–6,000 of which live outside Brazil (Dawson 2013: 5, 203 n. 21); the Italian organization, formally established in 2007, counts around 70 active members. Finally, Bambini di Satana was an Italian Satanist organization founded in 1982. At the apex of diffusion, it counted a few hundred members. It is now virtually defunct following the death of its founder in 2021.

Section 2 maps significant scholarly literature on NRMs and science. Sociologist William Sims Bainbridge published a seminal paper in 1993, encouraging colleagues to study the topic. Approximately twenty years later, academic engagement with NRMs and science blossomed. In 2010, Benjamin E. Zeller published *Prophets and Protons*, offering a perceptive analysis of three NRMs that utilized science in their worldview, as well as an abstract model for the science–religion relationship based on such analysis. In 2011, he edited a special issue of *Nova Religio*, the leading journal on the academic study of new religions, on NRMs and science. He reiterated that "scholars of new religious movements need to pay more attention to the ways adherents, leaders and founders of new religions use the idea of science" (Zeller 2011: 5); the issue carried four articles. The same year, James R. Lewis and Olav Hammer published their coedited, monumental *Handbook of Religion and the Authority of Science*, containing thirty-two essays, written by scholars with different academic backgrounds and methodologies, mostly including contributions on NRMs (Lewis & Hammer 2011).

Other articles have been published in different scholarly journals, and experts often reflect on the role of science in studies focusing on other aspects of the NRMs they specialize in. For the reconstruction of the scholarly conversation on NRMs and science, I selected the most significant or influential voices. I examine essays and monographs that identify general trends in the history of spirituality and new religions, or that advance typologies for the study of the relation between NRMs and science.

In Section 3, I wrap up the discussion, advancing proposals for future work on NRMs and science.

1 Five Case Studies

In 1950, the US pulp fiction writer Lafayette Ronald Hubbard (1911–86) published an article in a sci-fi magazine (Hubbard 1950a) as well as a voluminous book (Hubbard 1950b), that, drawing upon ideas he had been elaborating for more than a decade, introduced Dianetics, a self-improvement method presented as a "modern science of mental health." (The amount of scholarly literature and primary sources related to Hubbard, Dianetics, and Scientology is staggering. I elaborate here on investigations and reflections published in Bigliardi 2016. For a thorough scholarly reconstruction of the movement's history, see Urban 2011. See also Donald A. Westbrook's Element on Scientology studies in this series [Westbrook 2022a] and his monograph *Among the Scientologists* [Westbrook 2019].)

According to Hubbard, mnemonic traces of traumatic events, called engrams, encumber and obfuscate the human mind. It is, however, possible to identify and eliminate them through a procedure called auditing, leading to a dramatic improvement of one's mental and physical potential.

Later, Hubbard conceptualized the human soul as an entity, called thetan, that goes through successive incarnations but that also can forget its own potential for freedom and creativity. According to Hubbard, the history of the thetans, as verified through auditing, goes back seventy-six trillion years (Hubbard 2007b [1952]). Hubbard incorporated Dianetics in a teaching that he called Scientology, which offered to its followers, through a long and complex path called "Bridge to Total Freedom," to advance toward "higher states," including OT (Operating Thetan) levels. Individuals who reach the highest levels are said to have control over matter, energy, space, and time.

From a historical viewpoint, the Dianetics movement occurred from 1950 until the incorporation of the first Scientology churches in 1953. However, Dianetics and Scientology are separate subjects – the former (Hubbard's mental health system) being presented as the substudy and forerunner of the latter (Hubbard's applied religious philosophy). However, the lines between the two are at times blurred; most notably, the language and techniques of Dianetics show up in the OT levels.

Hubbard was initially looking for approval from the American Medical Association and the American Psychological Association, to which he unsuccessfully presented his theories. In fact, once such theories gained visibility they were deemed pseudoscientific and pseudomedical by the establishment. Hubbard started attacking psychology and psychiatry as unscientific and abusive. (It should be recalled that psychiatry back then resorted to practices such as lobotomy and electroshock therapy.) It is not unusual for Scientology to use anti-psychiatry campaigns and materials to attract potential affiliates. The museum *Psychiatry: An Industry of Death* was opened in Los Angeles in 2005, operated by Scientology's organization Citizens Commission on Human Rights (CCHR). The same name is used for similar touring exhibitions in the United States and internationally, and serves as the title of a documentary (Citizens Commission on Human Rights 2006). CCHR was cofounded in 1969 with Thomas Szasz (1920–2012), a psychiatrist highly critical of his own field, who in fact declared he was an atheist and not affiliated with Scientology (Westbrook 2017).

In the mid-1950s, Hubbard presented a device called the Electropsychometer, or E-Meter, as essential for auditing, a procedure that is usually (but not exclusively) performed by a subject seeking spiritual improvement, a preclear, and an auditor, who supervises and guides the procedure. Except for some levels of the "Bridge to Total Freedom" that do not routinely use the E-Meter, the device plays a crucial role in Scientology.

Hubbard emphasized that the E-Meter is irreplaceable and infallible. He wrote that "the E-Meter utterly dwarfs such inventions as that of the microscope" (Hubbard 1989 [1982]: 6). It is reported that Hubbard himself underwent auditing systematically, solo or with an auditor, keeping detailed records for years (Corydon & Hubbard 1987: 372; Miller 1987: 250).

In fact, the usage of a device for Dianetics had been proposed as early as 1951 by chiropractor and writer Volney G. Mathison (1897–1965), who belonged to Hubbard's circle. Hubbard initially resisted it, also claiming that it depersonalized the sessions, after Mathison's refusal to turn over the device's patent rights to him. However, he finally came up with his own version (1955) that was later patented (1966). There have been eight versions of the device so far, all redesigned and repatented. The latest one, called Mark VIII Ultra, was released in November 2013.

The E-Meter is a battery-powered machine composed of a principal box connected through cables to two electrodes in the form of metal cans. Once it is switched on, it sends a small electrical flow through the person who holds the cans. Variations in the flow result in the movements of a needle on the device's display.

Hubbard explained his views by using both a rich nomenclature of his own invention and terms and concepts of physics employed in an unusual way. For instance, he claimed that thought has a "mass" and a "resistance"; he wrote statements like the following: "The resistance of a dead female body is 5,000 ohms and of a dead male body, 12,500 ohms" (Hubbard 1983 [1966]: 3).

In standard physical terms, an E-Meter is based on a Wheatstone bridge, that is, a circuit that measures electrical resistance. This terminology is accepted by Hubbard; indeed, he and other Scientologists patented the E-Meter not by referring to it as a tool used for Dianetics/Scientology purposes but as a device that measures and indicates changes in resistance of a living body.[1] This, however, is integrated in Scientology teachings through Hubbard's own parlance and concepts, who asserted that the E-Meter reacts to electrical impulses generated by thought.

In fact, the name E-Meter notwithstanding, an auditor does not measure values but interprets the needle's movements as a consequence of questions regarding past incidents the preclear is asked about. The movement that is perhaps the most well known is the "floating needle," or F/N, described as "a

---

[1] Some examples: Patent US 3290589, December 6, 1966 (https://patents.google.com/patent/US3290589); Patent US 4459995, July 17, 1984 (https://patents.google.com/patent/US4459995); Patent US 4578635, March 25, 1986 (https://patents.google.com/patent/US4578635); Patent US 4702259, October 27, 1987 (https://patents.google.com/patent/US4702259).

rhythmic sweep of the needle on an E-Meter dial at a slow, even pace, back and forth, back and forth (. . .) mean[ing] that the charge on a subject being audited has dissipated, and [being] one of the indications of a process being complete" (Glossary of Scientology & Dianetics Terms 2000–2015). Hubbard's writings prescribe the procedure in great detail, including meticulous descriptions of the needle's possible behavior. Auditors are required to undergo intensive training in order to operate the device.

In a 1952 lecture, Hubbard compared the E-Meter and a polygraph: "The difference between this machine and a police department machine is elementary: a police department machine is just more of it. A police department machine measures respiration, blood pressure, [and] electronic impulse. [The E-Meter] measures solely the electrical resistance of the body" (Hubbard 2007a [1952]: 187). To this, he added: "But mind you, this machine has to be cared for. You have to take good care of the machine. And if you get one of your own, for heaven's sakes, don't let anybody else use it. It'll get so temperamental you won't even be able to talk to it" (Hubbard 2007a [1952]: 238). (This passage may give the impression that Scientologists aren't allowed to share meters. In practice, however, Scientologists in the church do sometimes borrow meters or share them for "co-auditing." There is no prohibition on sharing, as long as the member is in good standing [Westbrook 2022b, pers. comm.].)

E-Meter Essentials (Hubbard 2006 [1961]) emphasizes the device's irreplaceability. Hubbard wrote: "there is no known way to clear anyone without using a meter," and "there is no guarantee that scrap or nonstandard meter will behave properly." He stressed that the device requires constant practice: "The only way known to learn to use an E-Meter is use one, handle one, practice with one. Skill in meter use depends upon familiarizing oneself with the actual meter." In the same vein, Hubbard added: "Get familiar with the meter by holding it, watching it, turning it on and off. Touch it. Reach and withdraw from it. Play catch with it. Don't just read books about it." The E-Meter is described as infallible: "The person who says the meter is not a precision instrument is either unfamiliar with one or has something to hide. The auditor's questions can be off. The meter never is" (Hubbard 2006 [1961]: 9). The device is even said to "know" more than its users. "The meter registers *before* the preclear becomes *conscious* of the datum. It is therefore a pre-conscious meter" (Hubbard 2006 [1961]: 10, original emphasis). Moreover, Hubbard added, "[The E-meter] 'knows' more about the preclear than the preclear. It is reading created masses he is withholding himself from. The preclear won't confront all he is creating. Hence the omniscience of the meter" (Hubbard 2006 [1961]: 22).

Technology, or tech, is an important term in Scientology parlance. Its meaning encompasses Hubbard's discoveries and teaching, the vocabulary he uses to explain them, and their application. In other words, technology means Scientology's doctrine. As expressed in a 1965 document entitled "Keep Scientology Working," still used as an introduction to auditor training courses and displayed in the rooms of Scientology organizations, Hubbard was insistent on the preservation of standard tech, that is, Scientology's doctrines as established by him (Hubbard 1965). This function is currently fulfilled by the Religious Technology Center, directly run by Scientology's leader David Miscavige (b. 1960).

One important point is that Hubbard suggested that the truth of Scientology should be subjectively ascertained and confirmed. As he declared: "Nothing in Scientology is true for you unless you have observed it and it is true according to your observation" (Hubbard 1961).

In tune with the postwar climate, Hubbard also developed an interest in, and expressed concern about, radiation and its effects, publishing a book about the subject (Hubbard 1957). In 1958, the US Food and Drug Administration (FDA) confiscated and destroyed 21,000 Dianazene tablets, a supplement that, according to Hubbard, protected against radiation. In 1963, the Founding Church of Scientology in Washington, DC, was raided by US marshals acting on an FDA warrant and hundreds of E-Meters were confiscated. The FDA accused Scientology of falsely claiming that the device had therapeutic properties, both for physical and mental illnesses (Urban 2011: 62–3). Court battles dragged on for almost a decade. Finally, District Court Judge Gerhard Alden Gesell (1910–93), while denying medical validity to the device (and recognizing that it had been represented as a medical device), ordered the property to be returned to the Church and allowed its use in religious counseling. The Judge wrote "Here is a pseudo-science that has been adopted and adapted for religious purposes." From that time on, he ordered that all E-Meters

> should bear a prominent, clearly visible notice warning that any person using it for auditing or counseling of any kind is forbidden by law to represent that there is any medical or scientific basis for believing or asserting that the device is useful in the diagnosis, treatment or prevention of any disease. It should be noted in the warning that the device has been condemned by a United States District Court for misrepresentation and misbranding under the Food and Drug laws, that use is permitted only as part of religious activity, and that the E-meter is not medically or scientifically capable of improving the health or bodily functions of anyone.

The Judge added that "each user, purchaser, and distributee of the E-meter shall sign a written statement that he has read such warning and understands its contents and such statements shall be preserved." A warning notice similar to the E-Meter's one should feature in all literature referring to the E-Meter and auditing.[2]

Currently, Scientology uses this description:

> It is a religious artifact used as a spiritual guide in auditing. It is for use only by a Scientology minister or a Scientology minister-in-training to help the preclear locate and confront areas of spiritual upset. In itself, the E-Meter does nothing. It is an electronic instrument that measures mental state and change of state in individuals and assists the precision and speed of auditing. The E-Meter is not intended or effective for the diagnosis, treatment or prevention of any disease. (Church of Scientology International 2022a)[3]

Anti-Scientology authors and activists, including ex-members, are highly critical of the E-Meter, making different arguments against it. For example, although the E-Meter definitely detects a resistance, such resistance can hardly be identified with that created by the "mass" of "thoughts" (Cooper 1971; Jacobsen 2009). The resistance of the electric flow is heavily influenced by the strength with which the cans are held, the extension of skin in contact with them, sweat's salinity, and so on (Schafmeister, undated). Hubbard was not consistent in his descriptions of the E-Meter (Ortega 2014). The E-Meter is not worth its price (e.g., US$5,000–6,000 for a Mark VIII model), and the movement encourages auditors to own two units since one may break down (Jacobsen 2009; Ortega 2014). There also exist small groups of independent, or "Free Zone," Scientologists, who also make use of the E-Meter or their own variations, outside of church control (Thomas 2021).

Despite occasional suggestions that he was a "nuclear physicist" – for instance, on the dust jacket of the original edition of *All About Radiation* (Hubbard 1957) – Hubbard did not have academic or scientific credentials. He did try studying engineering at George Washington University, but he dropped after two years (1930–32). His grades in physics were particularly low. In the 1950s, he also used the title "doctor" that he had received from a diploma mill. However, in 1966 he issued a statement in which he renounced it, protesting against all those who, endowed with PhDs, had harmed humanity (Miller 1987: 255).

---

[2] See *United States of America* v. *Founding Church of Scientology et al.*, 333 F. Supp. 357 (D.D.C. 1971), §§ 363–5: https://law.justia.com/cases/federal/district-courts/FSupp/333/357/1606969/.

[3] It is worth adding that the label on the current model (full name: Hubbard Professional Mark Ultra VIII Electrometer) reads: "This electrometer is a religious artifact intended only for use by Scientology ministers, ministers-in-training and other qualified parishioners, as a guide in confessionals and counseling to help locate the source of spiritual travail. By itself this meter does nothing, and is neither medically or scientifically useful for the diagnosis, treatment or prevention of disease. *Ownership or use of this meter by anyone not in good standing with the Church of Scientology is prohibited*" (Westbrook 2016, pers. comm.; emphasis added).

In the introduction to his novel *Battlefield Earth*, Hubbard pointed out that "materialistic science" often "runs into (and sometimes adopts) such things as the Egyptian myth that man came from mud," adding "that there is another realm besides dedicated – and even simple-minded – materialism" (Hubbard 2005 [1982]: xviii). Elaborating on science fiction, he emphasized that, unlike fantasy, it must abide by standards of scientific credibility. He also stated that science fiction in its Golden Age (the 1930s to 1940s) had a mission and was avidly read by scientists, whom it inspired. He recalled an episode in which, while visiting "a major university's science department," he was recognized and congratulated by "professors and deans," adding that "for a while, before and after World War II, [he] was in rather steady association with the new era of scientists, the boys who built the bomb, who were beginning to get the feeling of rockets" (Hubbard 2005 [1982]: xix; see also Bigliardi 2017).

Hubbard's writings, as they currently are circulated among, and studied by, Scientologists, contain statements that involve medical notions. In *History of Man*, about a certain traumatic experience he stated: "when audited on a long series of people, [it] was found to eradicate such things as asthma, sinus trouble, chronic chills, and a host of other ills" (Hubbard 2007b [1952]: 103).

Scientology runs drug rehabilitation centers worldwide called Narconon. Founded in 1966, they operate on the basis of Hubbard's theory that toxins and drugs stored in adipose tissue can be eliminated through the so-called Purification Rundown. This method relies on sauna-induced perspiration and physical exercise as well as the consumption of vitamins and supplements (Westbrook 2022a: 12).

In interaction with the general public, such as in a 2014 TV Super Bowl advertisement, Scientology conjures up science and technology while displaying the E-Meter. In such advertisement, one would hear: "Imagine science and religion connecting. Imagine technology and spirituality combining. Now imagine that everything you ever imagined is possible. Scientology ... there are higher states of existence" (Scientology Spiritual Technology 2014).

Dianetics, Scientology, and Science: Commentary

Dianetics was presented by Hubbard as a science in the very title of the volume that introduced it. The term itself is reminiscent of fields like cybernetics, an expression defined and diffused by mathematician Norbert Wiener (1894–1964) after World War II. Scientology conjures up the very word science and utilizes a suffix typically denoting the systematic study of a subject or field. The term technology, suggesting scientific know-how, rather than dogma or doctrine, is used for Hubbard's teaching and established practices. Thus, the development of

Dianetics and Scientology is presented as discoveries similar to major break-throughs in science. Hubbard's teaching is expressed in a lingo presenting significant overlaps with the vocabulary of physics. The E-Meter is described, and appears, as a technological device that was even patented: a procedure that may be perceived as an external, official confirmation of its effectiveness. Dianetics and Scientology are regarded as therapeutic – their health-giving character is either explicitly claimed by Hubbard (at least, in some passages of his work) or implied by the overall, extraordinary psychophysical improvement they promise. Additionally, Hubbard had his own views and prescriptions regarding the physiology of drug addiction and of radiation poisoning.

Most likely, Hubbard perceived and presented Dianetics as both a science and as a therapeutic technique, being influenced by different factors, biographical as well as social and cultural. While conceiving of Dianetics, he may have been inspired by knowledge of Freudian psychotherapy acquired in informal exchanges, in particular, with Joseph "Snake" Thompson, a medical officer in the US Navy with whom he interacted in 1923 (Westbrook 2022a: 47). Unlike Freudian psychotherapy, Dianetics promised quick results, and it was an all-American product that could be received via mail and implemented on one's own. Fully a child of its epoch, Dianetics was, marketing-wise, the right product at the right time.

More generally, Hubbard felt and exploited the prestige of science typical of postwar United States. At the same time, he was also driven by, and capitalized on, science and technology-related fears typical of that very period, such as anxiety toward the use (or misuse) of atomic energy.

The fact that Hubbard tried to obtain recognition by psychiatry isn't neces-sarily a sign of cynicism on his part: he may not have realized that what he was advancing was a narrative rather than a testable theory that a scientific commu-nity could assess. Eventually, however, he was able to capitalize on the attacks his teachings received from scientific institutions, positioning himself as a competitor, superior to them in terms both of effectiveness and integrity.

For all these reasons, and as confirmed in the 2014 Super Bowl advertise-ment, Scientology is seen and proposed by adherents as a special science and technology. Its promised results in fact surpass those of ordinary technology and science, without the potentially destructive methods of fields like psychiatry. Hubbard also suggested that materialistic science is flawed; thus, anyone representing official science, and negatively assessing Scientology, can be considered by a Scientologist the representative of a discipline that is ultimately unfit, morally as well as methodologically, to evaluate Scientology itself. Additionally, Hubbard subjectivized the truth of Scientology in such a way that places it beyond falsification – if a practitioner tries it, and it works, then it is true for them. Moreover, the characterization of Scientology as a religion can be used to shield Dianetics and Scientology from science-based criticism. This manifested itself in the legal battle over the E-Meter, when Scientologists were given the possibility to retain it while emphasizing its pastoral function and formally dropping the therapeutic implications.

The E-Meter's design and its elements have been renewed over time. Critical scrutiny reveals an unresolved tension between Hubbard's claims about the E-Meter's infallibility and the idea that its updated versions represented an enhancement. But this is not too different from the subtle incongruity experienced within those religions in which a certain doctrine has to be presented as perfect and immutable while actually being adjusted to the challenges of a particular time. There also seems to be a symbolic dialectic at work: the E-Meter as a technological item is suggestive of objectivity, and as such it bestows rigor on the auditing procedure. Yet Hubbard's writings tend to personify the device, ascribing to it traits that are usually associated with a human being. Auditing appears both as a precise science and as an art. It has been argued that Hubbard's very presence is symbolically channeled through the E-Meter (Christensen 2009: 427 n. 53). In other words, the device extends in time and space the infallibility, the reliability, and the originality associated by Scientologists with Hubbard as the initiator, the first teacher of auditing, and the only individual fully versed in its use. It is no accident that the device's official name is actually the "Hubbard Electropsychometer."

In 2005, the French sociologist Régis Dericquebourg conducted a survey aimed at verifying whether Scientology members in France, while legitimizing their beliefs, resorted to the same arguments used in official literature. Dericquebourg observed that they would, for instance, mention tangible improvements in their life or state that Scientology is based on reliable technology, but they would not reference a perceived compatibility between Scientology and accredited science. Dericquebourg offered several explanations: maybe such compatibility was taken for granted to the point of not being talked about; members probably gave more importance to personal experience than to official literature; Scientology could be, in their minds, a replacement for science; also, at the time of the survey, Scientology was emphasizing its presentation as a religion (Dericquebourg 2011: 753). In 2009, Dericquebourg conducted a second survey, this time explicitly prompting Scientologists to state whether they thought that Hubbard's teachings were confirmed by science, and to elaborate on this point. The majority of the members who responded replied in the affirmative, but the arguments offered to integrate their answers were varied. Some of them, for instance, went rather off topic, reporting concrete improvements in their life. Other members pointed out that some aspects of Scientology were checked by science, including notions regarding the mind and brain, radiation, and the psychosomatic origin of diseases. Some described Hubbard's methods as scientific. Other members stated that they weren't well informed scientifically, or dismissed science as futile, or answered that Hubbard's teachings confirmed science. Dericquebourg observed, however, that those Scientologists who mentioned science to validate their creed did so in (vague) reference to popular perceptions of science rather than precise academic science (Dericquebourg 2011: 755–9).

The Raëlian Movement: History and Beliefs

The founder of the Raëlian Movement, Claude Vorilhon, was born in Vichy, Allier, in 1946. According to his own writings, he was raised in Ambert by a single mother. He believed his father to be Jewish; his mother, albeit Catholic, did not have him baptized (Vorilhon 1977a: 15, 23). Vorilhon attended Catholic schools and was neither a brilliant student nor very concerned with matters of faith (Vorilhon 1977a: 19–23). He developed a taste for poetry, speed, and autoeroticism early on (Vorilhon 1977a: 19–21). At the age of fifteen he headed to Paris where he started working as a singer (Vorilhon 1977a: 24ff). His dream was to become a race car driver. He became a sports journalist and later, having moved to Clermont-Ferrand, he established his own sports car magazine. Thanks to the improved financial situation and the contacts that this job brought him, he was able to purchase a race car and fulfill his dream (Vorilhon 1977a: 28–32; see also Palmer 2004 for additional biographical information).

In 1974, Vorilhon released a small book reporting an extraordinary experience that had occurred the year before. On December 13, while walking alone in an extinguished volcanic crater next to Clermont-Ferrand, he witnessed the landing of a spaceship from which emerged a diminutive, human-like, bearded figure, radiant and friendly (Vorilhon 1974: 17–19). On board the spaceship, Vorilhon received a revelation from the alien over a time span of six days, articulated in successive meetings that Vorilhon was expected to keep secret (Vorilhon 1974: 23).

The alien offered a narrative concerning the origin of humanity, but he also gave Vorilhon a mission. He presented himself as the exponent of a race called the Elohim, a name that he translated as "those who came from the sky" (Vorilhon 1974: 30). Such aliens created humanity 25,000 years ago using the Earth as a laboratory for biological experiments that they had previously been performing on their planet (Vorilhon 1974: 29). The Elohim themselves had similarly been created by another alien race, that also had been created in its turn, in a transmission chain whose infinity matches that of the universe in time and space; humans are just passages among innumerable others (Vorilhon 1974: 123). Human beings are to become aware of, and active in, such a chain of creations. This part of the revelation thus discloses that biological evolution was artificially produced – the birth of new species was determined and designed, and fossils are the remnants of terminated experiments (Vorilhon 1974: 125–7).

The Elohim have been monitoring humanity, orienting its growth toward a status of maturity in which humans can fully and consciously assume the role of creators. This has been done through prophets, the last of which is Vorilhon. With the name of Raël, meaning "light/ambassador of the Elohim" (Vorilhon 1974: 127), he shall spread the truth about humanity's origins, encourage fellow humans to correct the social order so as to stop inequality and injustice, and promote the construction of an embassy for the aliens in Israel. The completion of such embassy will function as an invitation to the aliens to replicate, on a global scale, the encounter they had with Vorilhon, the building being the tangible sign that humanity has fully understood where it comes from and where it is heading (Vorilhon 1974: 138–41; Vorilhon 1977a: 87–8).

The Elohim abolished physical work through technology (Vorilhon 1974: 148); they do not marry (Vorilhon 1974: 149). Among the Elohim's favorite ways to enjoy life is sex, and though sexual intercourse can lead to birth, they prefer to replicate themselves artificially. The replication consists of infusing consciousness into an artificial body (Vorilhon 1974: 147). The artificial bodies are extremely durable, lasting between 750 and 1,200 years. Immortality, however, is reserved to those Elohim who intellectually and morally excel (Vorilhon 1974: 147–8).

Vorilhon learned that his real father was the alien Yahweh, who also fathered Jesus, making Vorilhon Jesus's half-brother (Shamir 2020). He was conceived the same year of the bombings of Hiroshima and Nagasaki, 1945, from which the years should now be counted (Vorilhon 1974: 110–1). The reason why he is not endowed with special powers, such as performing miracles, is the unprecedented explicitness of the message. We live in the age of the apocalypse (i.e., revelation), and the Elohim manifest themselves for what they are. Spectacular events would distract people, running the risk of creating an old-fashioned religion (Vorilhon 1974: 154). Vorilhon is ideal as a prophet since, being neither a scholar nor a scientist, he can explain the message in lay terms (Vorilhon 1974: 22). However, he also feels that his capacities are artificially enhanced by the Elohim (Vorilhon 1977a: 37).

A crucial part of the exchanges between Vorilhon and the alien is an exegesis of the Bible, a copy of which he had felt compelled to buy in the days before the encounter and that he was invited to bring along (Vorilhon 1974: 20, 23). The alien presented the Bible as a fundamentally genuine record of human creation and of humanity's interaction with the Elohim. However, it was also explained that the records had been filtered through the consciousness of authors who were not equipped to understand the phenomena or events they were witnessing or transcribing (Vorilhon 1974: 30, 65). Therefore, the text has to be unwrapped from its naive literary aspects. When it refers to God, for example, it actually indicates the Elohim, and narratives of miracles are nothing but unsophisticated descriptions of technological devices and interventions that the Elohim used while interacting with humanity. Following this interpretation, references to technological devices can be detected behind highly symbolic Biblical artifacts and events. For instance, Noah's Ark was a spaceship used to preserve fauna and flora when the Elohim decided to punish humans for their misdemeanors (Vorilhon 1974: 38–41). Sodom and Gomorrah were destroyed with nuclear weapons, as the kind of physical damage suffered by Lot's wife (who was in fact turned into a pillar of salt) demonstrates (Vorilhon 1974: 43). The Ark of the Covenant was a device to communicate with the aliens; those who inappropriately tried to touch it electrocuted themselves (Vorilhon 1974: 60). Elijah was taken up in the skies on a flying device (Vorilhon 1974: 65). Jesus's walk on water was made possible by antigravity rays (Vorilhon 1974: 102). The resurrections or resuscitations were due to extremely advanced medicine (Vorilhon 1974: 96–7). The multiplication of the loaves and the fish was brought about by using synthetic food in the form of pills (Vorilhon 1974: 101). Jesus's parable of the sower is a metaphorical account of the successive attempts at creating living beings (Vorilhon 1974: 98–9). The alien suggested that Vorilhon could continue interpreting the text in similar vein, and that other sacred texts contain traces of truth (Vorilhon 1974: 120–1; Vorilhon 1977a: 150) although a great part of the Bible consists of worthless, uninformative "poetic babblings" (French, *bavardages*; Vorilhon 1974: 30).

On October 7, 1975, while alone and immersed in nature, Vorilhon was contacted again – this time to be taken to the Elohim's planet (Vorilhon 1977a: 49–50). There he was given more details about the way in which he had been monitored and guided since birth. He also met Moses, Elijah, Buddha, and Mohammed (Vorilhon 1977a: 73–4), and he got to know Elohim society in detail.

As a religious leader, Raël promotes two parallel messages. On the one hand, humans have to fully match the Elohim's technological and social advancement to earn contact with their creators. One fundamental measure to be taken is the establishment of a geniocracy, in which the citizens allowed to vote are those whose intelligence is 10 percent above average; still more intelligence is required (50 percent above average) to assume power (Vorilhon 1974: 132–4;

Vorilhon 1977b: 11). On the other hand, deserving individuals, upon their death, can be bestowed scientific resurrection on the Elohim's planet, their consciousness being infused into an artificial body that replicates their young one, provided that their cellular plan was transmitted to the Elohim in a ceremony performed by Raël or a Raëlian guide (Palmer 2004: 58–60; 84–5).

Raëlians are encouraged to keep themselves abreast of scientific advancements and a section in Raëlian websites fulfills this function. Raël sees science, synonymously with technology, as the instrument through which a paradise on earth can be created (Vorilhon 1977a: 62). "Science," he writes, "is the most important thing for men. You will keep yourself updated about all the scientists' discoveries that can solve all the problems." In fact, he presents science and religion as one and the same thing: "Science must be your religion. ... Being a scientist you please your creators, because you act like them and you show that you are aware of being made in their image" (Vorilhon 1977b: 131). In a Marx-flavored exhortation, scientists, together with philosophers and artists, are encouraged to get rid of the powers that try to manipulate them: "you who have always been exploited and betrayed by political and economic powers that transformed your inventions into deadly weapons and your art into propaganda for their ideologies: It is time to unite!" (Vorilhon 1977b: 107).

In the 1990s, cloning came to prominence in public and academic debates, and it became a narrative motif in science-fiction movies. Notably, *Jurassic Park*, Steven Spielberg's blockbuster motion picture depicting the consequences of cloning prehistoric animals, based on Michael Crichton's 1990 novel, was released in June 1993. The birth of the first mammal cloned from an adult somatic cell, Dolly the Sheep, at Roslin Institute, University of Edinburgh, occurred on July 5, 1997. Additionally, cloning was in the limelight in the 1990s in academia, where it was debated by both natural scientists and ethics specialists.

Raël claimed that cloning was the technique the Elohim had been describing since the time of the first revelation, when they explained how they reached immortality. In contrast to the questions or condemnations pronounced by other religions against human cloning, Raël presented his movement as an ideal home for scientists seeking absolute freedom of research and experimentation (Vorilhon 2001). In the years 2000 to 2001, the Raëlian Movement attracted attention worldwide while advertising collaboration with the company Clonaid that, under the direction of the French chemist Dr. Brigitte Boisselier (b. 1956), allegedly managed to create a human clone; no evidence was ever introduced to support this claim. Clonaid also maintains it developed an embryonic cell fusion device called RMX 2020 (Clonaid 2022).

In 2003, Dr. Boisselier was officially appointed as Raël's successor (Palmer 2004: 124). Interviewed by Yoav Shamir in 2020 for the documentary *The Prophet and the Space Aliens*, Dr. Boisselier, elaborating on the promise that one's consciousness will be downloaded in a newly cloned body, asserted:

> Cloning is essential in Raëlian philosophy. . . . It's part of our scriptures that one day we'll be able to clone ourselves and download the personality and become eternal that way. We don't promise eternity like other religions, apart from scientific eternity that we can reach. (Shamir 2020)

Asked about the Clonaid initiative, Boisselier stated that it had been a success in terms of communication, emphasizing that Raëlians "carry a message that is not comfortable . . . the cloning message was one of the most uncomfortable . . . and somehow the fact that it was not proven made it even more uncomfortable for some" (Shamir 2020; for more on the Clonaid affair, see Palmer 2004 & Helland 2007).

Raël and the Raëlians often discuss technological advances and connect them with Raëlian revelation. In the preface to *Yes to Human Cloning*, Daniel Chabot, a professor of psychology, writes that "science confirmed Raël's prophecies" (Vorilhon 2001: 33). Within the same book, Vorilhon takes up other contemporary technological developments, such as genetically modified food, presented as the solution to world hunger (Vorilhon 2001: 57), as well as nanotechnology, that in his opinion will bring about the end of money and labor (Vorilhon 2001: 69). Raëlians have been publicly advocating for genetically modified organisms, siding, for instance, with Monsanto corporation and calling on the Brazilian government to lift its ban on genetically modified crops (USA Today 2003).

In the 2000s, the religious/traditional practice of female genital mutilation started being debated and criticized globally. Raël began championing the anti-mutilation cause and announced the construction of a clitoris reconstructing "Pleasure Hospital" in Burkina Faso, through a nonprofit organization, Clitoraid, set up by the Raëlians. The initiative had on its side Dr. Marci Lee Bowers, a surgeon specializing in gender confirmation (who does not identify as a Raëlian). However, the Minister of Health of Burkina Faso denied permission to open the facility. Hosted by a local clinic, Dr. Bowers and her team managed to operate on multiple women before their licenses to work in Burkina Faso were canceled (Strickland 2008; Lloyd-Roberts 2014). Clitoraid met with criticism from different observers in regard to its communication and methods. Concerns voiced included its lack of rigorous evaluative practice regarding the surgery's effectiveness; the plan to construct its own hospital in Burkina Faso instead of supporting existing ones offering reconstructive surgery; and finally, the fact that Clitoraid officials did not consult with local communities and institutions and showed a lack of consideration of the local culture (Boynton 2013). Responding to criticism coming from a representative of the Catholic Church, Dr. Boisselier stated: "that's just surgery ... science. Who are they to give us lessons? They are the ones denying science" (Shamir 2020).

Anthropologist Debbora Battaglia observed that "the movement attracted, among others, mainstream scientists whose scientific work was an act of faith and whose spirituality was motivated by science." She added: "Showcased on the Raël.com web site are testimonials from nanotechnologists, mechanical engineers, chemists, biologists, psychologists." Battaglia's primary consultant was "a neuroscientist who, during the period of [her] online and offline research between 2001 and 2003 held a postdoctorate appointment at Harvard." She further noted that "some have lost their jobs or job prospects as a result of being Raëlian ... due to the prevailing perception in the scientific community (including transhumanists and bioethicists) that Raëlian scientists are alarmingly misguided" (Battaglia 2007: 154).

Yoav Shamir emphasizes in his documentary that the movement includes members with scientific credentials, such as a Japanese mathematics professor, Dr. Phylis Hetie, a Harvard postdoc studying stem cells, or even Dr. Boisselier, who boasts two PhDs in chemistry and, according to the documentary, "was a senior scientist." Prompted by the filmmaker to reflect on what she would do if one day Raël confessed that he made up his narratives, Dr. Hetie stated, "I would still say thank you. My life would have never been the same without what he taught me. I probably wouldn't be a scientist today if I wasn't a Raëlian." In fact, she didn't claim that the Raëlian message inspired in her a specific interest in science; however, she did suggest that she owed to the message a sense of freedom and the absence of inferiority complexes related to her skin color and gender (Shamir 2020).

Ex-Raëlian and anti-Raëlian activist Jiro Kambe recognizes that some Raëlians who joined the movement in their youth were prompted to study scientific subjects because of Raël's message. He adds that the message, however, is based on blind faith in Raël's encounters and in telepathic communication, and that it includes inconsistent and naive beliefs. Cloning, he remarks, does not ensure individual immortality. Additionally, he claims that Raël, believing that the end of the world was near, began discouraging members from embarking on intellectual pursuits (Bigliardi 2015b).

The Raëlian Movement and Science: Commentary

In Raël's earliest revelation, reference to contemporary science and technology is used to reconceptualize Jewish and Christian sacred scriptures, subverting their traditional understanding. This kind of exegesis has been called *interpretatio technologica* (Richter 2012). Unlike Hubbard, Raël has no background in creative or sci-fi writing. Nevertheless, his narrative resonates with those of authors who developed the sci-fi–related subgenre of ancient aliens, including Robert Charroux (1909–78) and Jean Sendy (1910–78) who were influential in Francophone popular culture in the 1970s (for more, see Stoczkowski 1999).

While elaborating on the revelation in later years, Raël proved able to exploit the public visibility of certain scientific topics and debates. A case in point is the connection he established between the narratives about the Elohim's recreation of humans on their planet and cloning, although such narratives were originally formulated in generic terms. In this sense, reference to science has been used by Raël to confirm the veracity of the Raëlian message, making it appear as prophetic.

Multiple scholars tackle the role of science and technology in Raël's message. Bryan Sentes and Susan J. Palmer examine Raëlian cosmology's "presumed immanence." The Raëlian reading of the Bible, they write, albeit presented as a "demythologization," is "a mythologization or mystification of science" (Sentes & Palmer 2000: 101). Christopher Helland remarks that "the scientific component remains as mythic and nonprovable as the original discourse [the Bible], becoming science fiction rather than science" (Helland 2007: 281). Carly Machado states that "Raëlian cosmology is 'in between' themes of science fiction, religious desire, scientific innovation and contemporary social questions" (Machado 2010: 194). Machado speaks as well of a "sacralization of science" (Machado 2010: 201). (For further critical discussion see Bigliardi 2015a.)

Raël also encourages humans to enjoy current technological and scientific progress to the fullest. At the same time, he inspires them to push that very progress, so as to reach technoscientific development comparable to that of the Elohim, thus assuming the role of creators. The reward for individual Raëlians, including those who may not live long enough to see humanity's full upgrade on earth, is virtual immortality on the Elohim's planet, within a society that is characterized by ubiquitous technology allowing a hedonistic lifestyle. In sum, science and technology, according to Raël, carry the promise of a radical improvement of the human condition be it on earth or in an extraterrestrial afterlife, similarly to ideas advanced within nineteenth-century positivism, or even of immortality, analogously to twentieth- and twenty-first-century transhumanism.

Finally, Raël also presents his movement as the ideal home for scientists, whom he represents as restrained and exploited by the establishment. In fact, he suggests revolutionizing politics and society by making the possession of above-average intelligence the essential requirement for the management of power. Raël's protective attitude toward scientists has become apparent (and has, to a limited extent, met with success) in initiatives such as Clonaid and Clitoraid, when individuals with legitimate scientific credentials have been welcomed and supported by the movement. This also strengthens public perception of the Raëlians as scientific.

Unlike Scientology, the science and technology that the Raëlian Movement integrates into its teachings is not presented as something that the group already or exclusively possesses and practices, but as lying in the (near) future of humanity, or as being currently elaborated and developed by the scientific community. In other words, the Raëlian Movement does not promote a fully autonomous body of beliefs, practices, and devices presented as scientific; it rather tries to incorporate science and technology. However, the Raëlians can be challenged by critics for making overstatements about science and technology, such as the claims that cloning can lead to individual immortality (cf. Kambe 2012), or unfounded statements, such as the claims regarding generating the first human clone.

Finally, the Elohim's revelation doesn't fully deny the existence of evolution as a natural mechanism but describes it as having been boosted by alien intervention; additionally, Rael explains the fossil record in reference to alien experiments. This is a form of creationism that, as such, can be rejected as pseudoscientific or as ultimately clashing with Raël's overall appreciation of, and invitation to, science.

Falun Gong: History and Beliefs

Li Hongzhi, the founder of Falun Gong, was born in China in 1951, according to the movement (for a discussion of the different versions of his biography see Penny 2003). From childhood he studied with Buddhist and Daoist masters and he showed astonishing faculties, including levitation and invisibility. Shortly after turning thirty, he started fusing and systematizing into Falun Gong the doctrines and practices he had been learning until then. One main component of such doctrines and practices was Qi Gong, of which Li Hongzhi was a master, which encompassed powerful healing abilities. (Fuller discussions of Qi Gong's and Falun Gong's history, beliefs, and practices appear in Chen 2003; Palmer 2007; Ownby 2008; & Penny 2012.)

Qi Gong has a complex history. Qi denotes an energy, or vital spirit, and Gong stands for practice. Qi Gong is, in fact, a label that was applied in the 1950s to a bundle of practices and beliefs that had existed in China for millennia. In a nutshell, Qi Gong is a set of breathing exercises or techniques to be practiced in an open space, aimed at improving one's psychological and physical welfare. Such techniques stem from traditional Chinese medicine, martial arts,

Buddhism, and Daoism. The theory used to explain their benefits invokes the unity of mind and body. Following Mao Zedong's (1893–1976) communist revolution, such practices were institutionalized, including reference to them through scientific language. The communist government ascribed enormous importance to science for progress. Qi Gong was widespread and appreciated, also among revolutionaries, who therefore opted for a "normalizing approach" instead of eradicating it as superstitious and obsolete. Also, Qi Gong's promised benefits were appealing, considering the inadequate state of the healthcare system. In 1979, a scientist declared that Qi was a physical, measurable substance (Ownby 2008: 58–61). Between 1979 and 1980, efforts were made to reproduce and exploit physical Qi, including Qi-emitting devices and Qi anesthesia (Palmer 2007: 67).

After China's transition to a market economy (from the late 1970s onward), Qi Gong boomed for various reasons. Psychophysical enhancement was regarded as advantageous in a competitive society. Social interaction among practitioners was perceived as a source of stress relief. Additionally, Qi Gong could bring profits as a commercial enterprise. During the so-called "Qi Gong Fever" (in the 1980s and 1990s), practitioners started gravitating around charismatic leaders who were attributed supernatural and spectacular abilities.

In response, the Chinese government set out to coordinate and control Qi Gong groups in an official state association. Adherence to scientific standards was utilized as part of compliance with governmental concerns for practitioner safety and regulating self-proclaimed masters; those masters who resisted were denounced as practitioners of superstitious witchcraft or as pseudoscientific quacks (cf. Chen 2003: 72–5). Even the US-based CSICOP (Committee for the Scientific Investigation of Claims of the Paranormal, composed of scientists and professional magicians) was involved: following an investigation of Qi Gong masters in China, a negative assessment written by CSICOP was reported by a national weekly newspaper (Ownby 2008: 166–7).

Falun Gong can be described as an offshoot of Qi Gong, yet its practitioners emphasize its distance from the former, underscoring that it is a spiritual doctrine (Palmer 2007: 219–20). Falun Gong encompasses a worldview and ethical system based on truth, compassion, and tolerance, or forbearance of tribulations and ordeals. The term Falun refers to the wheel of the law. In Buddhist thought, law, or dharma, is a universal principle to learn and embrace. The wheel (of dharma) symbolizes the way the universe moves as well as the doctrine's perfection. In Falun Gong, however, wheels are distinctly meant as physical, energetic, and spinning ones that are located in the abdomen and that can be inserted in the body by the master or acquired through individual practice. They are described as multicolored and shiny and said to have a concrete effect on the practitioner's life and well-being. Additionally, the wheels are claimed to be observable only in a parallel universe or superior reality (Ownby 2008: 91, 120; Penny 2012: 5, 95–6, 188–93).

Li Hongzhi refers as well to a black substance or karma that causes illnesses, but that, if adequately treated through Falun Gong, can be dispelled or transformed into a white substance that practitioners declare they can feel. It is also believed that, through prolonged and intensive practice, or by the master's intervention, a practitioner can become fully disease-free through the complete eradication of pathogenic energy, a state called milk-white body (Palmer 2003: 352; Penny 2012: 127, 171–2, 187–8).

The master teaches and practices the refusal to display supernatural powers just for the sake of spectacularism (Penny 2012: 179). Moreover, he has prohibited practitioners from curing illnesses since 1995 (Penny 2012: 43). That being said, multiple practitioners do offer testimonials of the master's superhuman abilities and report marvels associated with his presence, including the apparition of dragons in the sky (Penny 2012: 40). Social scientists have collected accounts of Falun Gong-related healings among practitioners – including from illnesses such as cancer, diabetes, and tuberculosis – some of whom were even eager to show supporting medical documentation (Palmer 2003; Ownby 2008: 142, 145, 152). "Malaysian volunteers report that most practitioners are initially attracted to the movement for health reasons" (Ackerman 2005: 501).

Falun Gong began facing strong opposition by the Chinese government after spring 1999, following a peaceful demonstration by its practitioners in front of the headquarters of the Chinese Communist Party in Beijing (April 25). A couple of weeks earlier, practitioners had protested in meditation posture around Tianjin Normal University's administrative building; an article in a magazine published by said university had criticized the movement including allegations that its meditation practices could result in psychiatric illness (Palmer 2007: 266–7). Falun Gong was declared illegal in July the same year. Chinese authorities made specific accusations:

> "Falun Gong is an evil cult"; it is harmful to the physical and mental well-being of the people; it hurts society by disrupting social order and the work of institutions; it is superstitious and antiscience, hypocritical, criminal, treasonous, seditious, and well-organized. ... Chinese authorities claimed innumerable cases of the psychological and physical well-being of people being threatened by Falun Gong participants giving specific examples of alleged suicides supposedly caused by the Falun Gong. (Sacco 2011: 72)

In 1996, Li Hongzhi had left China for the United States, from where he toured the world lecturing and promoting Falun Gong. The very difficulties encountered by Falun Gong in China were conceptualized by him in the framework of an apocalyptic worldview. He started teaching that the world is about to be destroyed, just to be recreated anew, and it is being contested among good and evil forces.

Some of the evil forces are, according to Li Hongzhi, sinister extraterrestrials whose plan is to invade earth, since they covet human bodies. In fact, both humans and aliens were created by the gods, but aliens were left unsurveilled, multiplied, and degenerated (Li 1998a); human bodies, however, are still perfect (Dowell 1999). Some aliens abduct humans and perform cruel experiments on them on their planets (Li 1998a); other ones live on earth in disguise (Li 1998c). They use clones to replace human beings – a cloned body has no soul, it's not controlled by the gods, and can therefore be occupied by an alien (Li 1999). Alien presence on earth has been detected multiple times, especially through UFO sightings (Li 1997: 27). Such aliens have introduced modern science and technology to earth, including computers and airplanes (Dowell 1999). One sign of their presence is the extraordinary scientific and technological progress of the twentieth century, the development of computers in particular (Li 1998c). Gods, in addition to aliens, have steered or conditioned technological and scientific development on earth. One god, for instance, was sent down to ancient China to invent papermaking, while another god invented the compass (Li 1998b). Humankind, according to Li Hongzhi, has become spiritually and culturally dependent on science; in this sense, it can be said to already be controlled by aliens (Dowell 1999). Science and technology in fact have become indispensable and are to some extent advantageous; Li Hongzhi thus specifies that he is not against science (Dowell 1999). Science, however, is unequipped to study the dimensions and beings Falun Gong teaches about, and therefore induces a materialistic mindset that distracts people from the truth. He argues that science can neither detect fundamental spiritual dynamics (like changes in karma) nor can it prove the existence of heavenly paradises, both of which are essential, in his view, for understanding the meaning of human life and reaching salvation. In science, one "perceives materially," while in religion one "believes spiritually." For him, science's lack of vision also explains why scientists deem his teachings mere superstitions (Li 1998a). Furthermore, he points out that technology results in environment-destroying pollution, although he suggests that the gods played a role in the damage to the ozone layer (Li 1999). In sum, science and technology, according to Li Hongzhi, are powerful tools employed by aliens to keep humanity in a state of weakness and subjugation. Specific methods that aliens use to control terrestrials include keeping a register of all humans who can operate a computer (Li 1998a), and creating a layer of cells (or particles) in almost every single human body or brain that can be used to negatively affect an individual's thinking (Li 1998a; Dowell 1999). Such a layer, however, can be eliminated by the master, who is constantly engaged in fighting off aliens; in fact he reassures his followers that aliens are in the process of being completely eliminated (Li 1998a). (For more on Li Hongzhi's alien narratives, see Bigliardi 2019; on aliens in Falun Gong and their role in Li Hongzhi's cosmology, see also Farley 2014.)

Li Hongzhi teaches that practitioners can develop a supernormal ability, the celestial eye, allowing them to see the essence of things. While elaborating on this point, the master offers an explanation of ordinary sight as involving the optic nerves and the pineal gland (Penny 2012: 202–3). He also explains gravity by resorting to the concept of Three Realms that compose the universe – Heaven, Earth, and the Underworld – claiming that particles move across the Realms. "The theory of gravity science believes in nowadays," he states, "is totally wrong" (Li 2001: 19). Based on Li Hongzhi's cosmology and on their visions of the earth's past, practitioners also challenge the theory of evolution (Clear Wisdom Net 2001). Li Hongzhi resorts as well to a narrative according to which there exists a trilobite fossil with a human footprint on it left by a person wearing shoes. This, in his opinion, is evidence against scientific chronologies of human evolution since trilobites disappeared 260 million years ago (Li 2018: 21). Finally, he also declares that the moon was built by prehistoric humans, that it is hollow, and that ocean floors are inhabited by humanoids (Li 1996).

Falun Gong, Science and Technology: Commentary

Scholar Helen Farley emphasizes that there exists a "problematic discourse ... between Falun Gong and the scientific community," adding that it is "ironic given that the movement is so heavily reliant on the science of telecommunications to spread its word" (Farley 2011: 141). Falun Gong expert David Ownby points out that Li Hongzhi manages both to capitalize on science, where it carries an aura of prestige and modernity, and to express mistrust toward science's alleged shortcomings and limitations in comparison with the superior teachings of Falun Gong, and the superior knowledge Li Hongzhi himself is endowed with, whose nature he does not completely disclose (Ownby 2008: 98–102).

Falun Gong's inclusion of scientific concepts and language clearly appears to have been shaped and nourished by political, social, and cultural trends that characterized the rise of modern China. Falun Gong's scientific-sounding claims and references inherit the scientific attributes that Qi Gong was assigned in the earliest phase of the communist revolution and reflect, more generally, the importance ascribed to science by Chinese governmental authorities.

At the same time, Falun Gong may convey the idea that it is competing with science, in particular by promising psychophysical achievements that are comparable or superior to those of ordinary physical training and medicine. Not unlike Scientology, Falun Gong is suspected by its critics and detractors of dissuading practitioners from pursuing proper medical treatment in favor of Falun Gong's curative claims. Neglect of standard treatment may additionally be inspired by the doctrine's specific emphasis on forbearance toward suffering as a way to reduce karma (Ownby 2008: 110; cf. also Penny 2012: 180).

Important entities in Falun Gong's teaching, such as the wheels, while being ascribed tangible effects, are conceptualized in a way that makes them experimentally unverifiable. Additionally, Li Hongzhi's teaching is presented as a form of knowledge that is overall superior to science while being similar to it due to its systematic and research-based nature. In this case, the analogies with Scientology's teachings are strong.

Falun Gong may also be said to clash with science since it includes narratives about miracles. Such narratives are ambivalent, however. On the one hand, they defy science, strengthening the idea that Falun Gong carries knowledge and possibilities that surpass those accessible and available to ordinary scientists. On the other hand, Falun Gong also suggests that at least some extraordinary phenomena can ultimately be achieved through structured learning, which again contributes to the idea that Falun Gong ultimately is a science in its own right.

Li Hongzhi has no background in creative or sci-fi writing. However, his narratives regarding UFOs, aliens and paranormal phenomena resonate with pop-culture tropes of the 1980s and 1990s. He may well have been exposed to Chinese versions of books by ancient-aliens author Erich von Däniken (b. 1935) or the television series *X-Files* (Penny 2012: 132–3).

So far, the relation between Falun Gong and science has revealed imitational, competitive, and conflictual elements. Even more subtlety emerges if one scrutinizes Li Hongzhi's discourses about aliens. First, science and technology are "otherized" by ascribing their invention to nonhuman agents, including gods and extraterrestrials. Second, they are demonized by presenting them as tools through which evil forces manipulate human beings. Third, they are devalued by describing them as reliant on a limited understanding of reality – an idea that also allows Li Hongzhi to explain why rationalists may disparage or snub Falun Gong. Fourth, Li Hongzhi does admit that science and technology are not dispensable, but fifth, he suggests that all the evils related to science, technology, and aliens are ultimately kept in check by him, thus fostering his own charisma.

Critics also note that Falun Gong clashes with science through Li Hongzhi's teachings regarding the physiology of human sight, gravity, and evolution. His blunders in regard to science have been blamed on his lack of a solid education, especially in relevant fields (he is a junior high school graduate). Practitioners in rural areas of China are intellectually unequipped to detect and challenge the master's scientific misconceptions (Farley 2011: 155, 159). It has been observed, nonetheless, that many Chinese practitioners in North America have advanced degrees (Palmer & Ownby 2000). Some of such practitioners explicitly state that the master's teachings about science helped them to contextualize it within a cosmological vision, thus enabling them to see science's relevance for them and making full sense of it (Ownby 2008: 96–7).

Santo Daime/Stella Azzurra: History and Beliefs

In 1998, Walter Menozzi (b. 1975), an Italian exchange student in Brazil, happened to interact with a Santo Daime community in Rio de Janeiro. Santo Daime is a world religion of Brazilian origin that makes use of the brewed drink known as ayahuasca as a sacrament. Menozzi embraced it and decided to continue its practice in his native country, ending up playing a crucial role in the religion's diffusion in Europe, where he became a household name. In this process Santo Daime, as represented by Menozzi and conceptualized in his writings, significantly interacted with science in multiple ways. (For a history of Stella Azzurra's practices and controversies, see Bigliardi 2018; 2020.)

Santo Daime stems from the experience and teaching of Raimundo Irineu Serra (1890–1971), or Mestre (Master) Irineu, an Afro-Brazilian rubber worker who was raised in a folk Catholic environment. From native Amazonians he learned about the use of ayahuasca, a blend obtained from the decoction of a vine (*Banisteriopsis caapi*) and the leaves of a shrub (*Psychotria viridis*) that grow in the forest. Those who drank it were provided with strength and visions. In one such vision, Mestre Irineu was approached by a female spirit whom he identified as the Virgin Mary and the Queen of the Forest. He became famous as a healer, and the hymns he received during his visions were incorporated in Santo Daime ceremonies. The name Daime, used in reference both to the religion and the beverage, means "give me" – it was frequently heard by him in such experiences, and it is an exhortation to ayahuasca to bestow wisdom and other boons on those who ingest it in a ritual context. (For a thorough reconstruction of Santo Daime's history and beliefs, see Dawson 2013. See also Blainey 2021.) Detractors often describe ayahuasca as a hallucinogenic drug, but religious leaders and affiliates consider it a sacrament or entheogen. (See Richards 2015 on entheogens in general.) When consumed in a religious and ceremonial context, the mixture brings about deeply transformative experiences, in which one interacts with, or has feelings of intuition about, alternate or superior realities, spiritual entities, or one's true self.

Santo Daime in its current form continues the teaching and practices of either Mestre Irineu's group or of some other one deriving from a branching process that started after the founder's death. Menozzi first became familiar with entheogen-related narratives in 1997 through reading Terence McKenna's book *True Hallucinations: Being an Account of the Author's Extraordinary Adventures in the Devil's Paradise* (McKenna 1993). In Brazil, he got in touch with a group led by Padrinho Alfredo Mota de Melo (b. 1950), son of Padrinho Sebastião (1920–90), Mestre Irineu's most notable disciple. Menozzi stated that, before his experiences with Santo Daime, he was an atheist (Menozzi 2020, pers. comm.). In fact, Menozzi wasn't the first Italian to ever adopt Santo Daime or bring it to Italy. Upon his return from Brazil he joined a small community in Assisi that had been founded by Santo Daime practitioners who had interacted with Brazilian communities in the early 1980s.

Santo Daime ceremonies, or *trabalhos espirituais* (spiritual works), can last several hours and are open to nonmembers upon request, following individual scrutiny by experienced practitioners. They are celebrated regularly, according to a specific calendar. Those who officially want to commit to Santo Daime receive a uniform (*farda*) to be donned during rituals. In such ceremonies, women and men are separated. They stand or sit around a table, on which is placed the Cross of Caravaca (a cross with two horizontal bars) as well as other symbols, including the founders' pictures. The rituals are led by a *comandante* (male or female) who marks their salient moments with invocations or leads the singing of the hymns that are accompanied with maracas and other instruments. Ayahuasca is administered individually by the comandante and their aides. The participants stand in line to wait for their turn, similar to the administration of the Host during Catholic mass. The brew is poured from a carafe or a bottle into a small glass in a quantity decided by the comandante or their aide by looking at the participant and being inspired by the Daime itself.

In 2004, upon returning from a journey to Brazil, Menozzi was stopped at Perugia Airport with twenty-seven liters of ayahuasca. Up until that moment, he only had imported small quantities, provided with a phytosanitary certificate issued by the Brazilian Ministry of Agriculture, but due to some impasse, the document wasn't available that time. Italian authorities performed chemical analyses that ascertained the presence of dimethyltryptamine (DMT), classified as a Schedule I substance by the United Nations Convention of Psychoactive Substances (1971). That is, it was deemed to have strong potential for abuse and no accepted medical use. Menozzi was arrested and briefly jailed over accusations of criminal association and international drug trafficking. The arrest and subsequent trial of Menozzi, who was kept under house arrest, as well as of other practitioners, were covered by local and national press that described ayahuasca as a hallucinogenic drug, the rituals as orgiastic, and the movement as satanic.

While under house arrest, Menozzi wrote a monograph titled *Ayahuasca: La Liana degli Spiriti – il sacramento magico-religioso dello sciamanismo amazzonico* (Ayahuasca: The Vine of the Spirits – The Magic-religious Sacrament of Amazonian Shamanism). First published in 2007, it is written in a confessional vein but with an impersonal style. Menozzi does not report on his own experiences with ayahuasca, and when he touches upon the challenges he encountered, he narrates them in the third person singular. Additionally, he cites academic and scientific literature.

The book opens with a reference to natural science: "From the 1950s onwards, the scientific knowledge of the botany and chemistry of psycho-active plants has developed enormously" (Menozzi 2013 [2007]: 13). Menozzi discusses the separation between "medicine, psychology, and religious spirituality" in Western society (Menozzi 2013 [2007]: 18). Drawing upon ideas advanced by the US psychologist Ralph Metzner (1936–2019) in a 1993 article entitled "The Split Between Spirit and Nature in European Consciousness," Menozzi notes that major Western scientists and thinkers, such as Newton, Galileo, and Descartes, were forced to posit a separation between science and religion to bypass the Church's domination and persecution. This resulted in discrediting subjective experiences. Such a fracture, he argues, can be cured by reviving shamanic traditions (Menozzi 2013 [2007]: 19–20). At the end of the book, he emphasizes that his discussion is not marked by a negative judgment over reason. "On the contrary," writes Menozzi, "it is a denunciation of reason's very decline and subservience to the pretensions of cultural and cognitive ethnocentrism" (Menozzi 2013 [2007]: 302).

Menozzi describes the substances contained in ayahuasca through accurate chemical language. *Banisteriopsis caapi* carries harmine, harmaline, and tetra-hydroharmine, alkaloids known as β-carbolines; *Psychotria viridis* carries the aforementioned DMT. Such substances, underlines Menozzi, are also naturally produced by the human body. Furthermore, the hallucinogenic effect is not due to DMT alone: β-carbolines inhibit some enzymes in the digestive system that would otherwise metabolize DMT. Menozzi emphasizes that the awareness of this synergy among indigenous Amazonians is a mystery (Menozzi 2013 [2007]: 28).

Menozzi reconstructs as well the biography of Padrinho Sebastião, recalling that Mestre Irineu healed him of a disease seemingly caused by an insect. The healing process involved an "intense cure" and a "spiritual operation on his body" (*operazione*, the Italian term, like the English one, can also refer to surgery) that Sebastião "witnessed from outside [of his body]" (Menozzi 2013 [2007]: 125). Menozzi also asserts that the ritual sessions of Santo Daime are to be seen broadly as curative, and that Padrinho Sebastião specifically designed some of them to heal ill people, including on a one-on-one basis (Menozzi 2013 [2007]: 132). He points out that ayahuasca can be used not only as a specific remedy for illnesses but also as a diagnostic instrument (Menozzi 2013 [2007]: 76). Additionally, he employs expressions such as "energetic organism" and "current" (Menozzi 2013 [2007]: 129, 131) when referring to the feelings and effects experienced during the spiritual works.

Menozzi challenges the way in which authorities the world over define certain substances as "drugs" and criminalize them, pointing out a major inconsistency – not all substances that alter consciousness and cause addiction are prohibited by different governments (Menozzi 2013 [2007]: 232). He is also careful, however, to distinguish ayahuasca and its ingestion in a ceremonial setting from such substances and their consumption. He stresses that of ayahuasca is not addictive; on the contrary, trained practitioners need lower and lower quantities to obtain the same result (Menozzi 2013 [2007]: 202). Additionally, he emphasizes that ayahuasca is effective in the treatment of drug and alcohol addiction and that it strengthens one's ethical inclinations (Menozzi 2013 [2007]: 205, 212–21). The very fact that ayahuasca can have strong side effects like vomit and diarrhea (interpreted by practitioners as spiritual cleansing) discourages its recreational usage (Menozzi 2013 [2007]: 134).

In court, Menozzi's defense initially presented a set of documents including scientific ones, and argued that Santo Daime did not feature in the list of the substances that are forbidden in Italy. The Court rejected the argument, pointing out that the brew is a mixture of two plants (as opposed to a natural product) that contains DMT, which is prohibited. However, Menozzi won the appeal with the Supreme Court. His defense argued that the preparation didn't contain more alkaloids than the original plants, which are not forbidden in and of themselves. In 2006, the case was dismissed.

In 2007, Menozzi set up the Santo Daime center Stella Azzurra, serving as its spiritual leader, president, and legal representative. He also serves as legal representative of ICEFLU Italia, a confederation of Italian Santo Daime groups. Menozzi chose the name Stella Azzurra (blue star) between 2008 and 2009 in reference to a recurring image in his Daime-related experiences since 2001.

A major setback for Italian Santo Daime practitioners occurred in early 2022, when the Italian government issued a decree including ayahuasca as well as *Banisteriopsis caapi* and *Psychotria viridis* in the list of forbidden substances.

In a participant observation I made in 2016 of a spiritual work (Bigliardi 2018) during informal interactions with the other participants – newcomers and experienced affiliates alike – I could frequently detect medical undertones in the description of the effects of ayahuasca or the discussion of expectations associated with consuming the brew. On one occasion, someone mentioned a leader in the Netherlands who was said to have been able to stop her cancer from developing and allowed her to survive for many years by rejecting official therapies and relying only on Daime. Menozzi later emphasized that he is aware of ayahuasca's healing properties (including kidney-stone disappearance and cancer remission), but he does not use them to promote Santo Daime. Additionally, even though he does not keep a detailed record of such episodes, he is confident that such results would be accepted by the medical community (Menozzi 2016, pers. comm.)

Before the formal start of the ceremony, new participants were requested to fill in a questionnaire, in which they were asked whether they were taking antidepressants and/or whether they were under treatment for hyperthyroidism. Those taking antidepressants were forbidden to participate, while those receiving treatment for hyperthyroidism were warned that their medicines could interfere with ayahuasca and intensify its effects.

"There is no physical or spiritual disease that cannot be cured through Santo Daime," declared Menozzi in his capacity as comandante during the spiritual work. Later, however, he would explain such a statement symbolically, in reference to Santo Daime as a spiritual doctrine and practice, not as a substance. Menozzi added his conviction that the origin of most diseases is psychosomatic and that they can be cured through adequate spiritual practice. He was also careful to specify that the aforementioned claim about physical and spiritual healing is not part of the standard ritual (Menozzi 2016, pers. comm.).

Stella Azzurra and Science: Commentary

In Menozzi's vision, science and Daime are related in multiple, intertwined ways. At first glance, one can identify analogies between his belief system and those respectively advanced by L. Ron Hubbard and Li Hongzhi. For instance, as in Scientology, ayahuasca-related experience is presented as tangible and, at the same time, subjective, that is, concretely verifiable through individual practice. One of Padrinho Alfredo's hymns describes Daime as a "teacher of teachers." It is said to convey a form of knowledge that is ultimately superior to that of science; similar claims are made by Li Hongzhi about his own teaching. Not unlike Scientology and Falun Gong practice, the sacrament is described as bearing health-related benefits while stressing that the real, most relevant improvement attainable through Santo Daime ultimately concerns a practitioner's spiritual level. Another similarity is the use of scientific terminology, including terms like energies and currents. It should be emphasized, however, that one fundamental principle of Daime is to never invite or coax people to come, and instead to trust that only people who are personally called out of their own free will are meant to attend the rituals.

The linguistic scientification of Daime may date back to the blending of Mestre Irineu's original teaching with nineteenth-century spiritual discourses including esotericism (Meyer 2013) and spiritism. As frequently mentioned in Menozzi's monograph, Sebastião Mota de Melo was familiar with Allan Kardec's (1804–69) spiritism when he approached Mestre Irineu. However, one should consider as well that the discussion of entheogens was later taken up by New Age authors who resorted to scientific nomenclature including energy and vibrations.

That being said, Menozzi's discourse about science also presents a degree of complexity and refinement exceeding that of the other doctrines considered so far. To fully appreciate it, one should first recall his background at the time he embraced Santo Daime and the circumstances in which his interest in ayahuasca and science unfolded. At the time of his Brazilian exchange, Menozzi was studying Economy and Finance at the prestigious Bocconi University (Milan), from which he would graduate in 1999. Arguably, higher education made him familiar with, and appreciative of, clear writing and structured arguments. In his monograph, he offered a confessional discourse incorporating information from academic sources, including articles by natural scientists. Additionally, Menozzi found himself compelled to explain ayahuasca to a large public at a moment when his religion was literally on trial. To be sure, Santo Daime was being publicly debated – indeed slandered – by sensationalist news articles casting doubts on its legitimacy and credibility as a religion. However, the central question in the trial concerned the brew's exact nature in relation to norms that invoked precise chemical language and classifications. Inevitably, the discussion in court had to be conducted by all parties with reference to scientific data and documents. Ultimately, the defense's ability to counter the prosecutor's description of ayahuasca with a likewise scientifically acceptable one was decisive in determining Menozzi's success in the trial.

I have recalled the analogy between the distribution of ayahuasca during a Santo Daime spiritual work and the Catholic eucharist. The Catholic belief that bread and wine, following the appropriate ritual, transform into Jesus's flesh and blood, does not ordinarily correspond with sensorial experience; in other words, while being consumed during the ritual, bread and wine simply look and taste like bread and wine, except in extraordinary cases. The miracle of the eucharist thus lends itself to doubt and criticism on behalf of empiricist observers; however, the *Catechism of the Catholic Church* conceptualizes the transformation as being beyond sensorial experience and rational comprehension while also emphasizing its reality.[4] (Other Christian denominations interpret the bread and wine symbolically.) A Santo Daime practitioner does not experience any such challenge; their sacrament does bring about an extraordinary yet very tangible experience. Moreover, Menozzi resorts to scientific literature to describe the very real effect of ayahuasca on the brain's physiology, with references to chemistry and its nomenclature.

Menozzi suggests that the effects of ayahuasca can be interpreted and conceptualized both from the viewpoint of Western, contemporary chemistry and physiology and from the viewpoint of shamanism. In his view, the two perspectives can and should be integrated, being, in fact, two different ways of looking at the same reality. Showing considerable intellectual acuity, Menozzi describes the fracture between religion and science – or between the subjective and the objective knowledge of reality – as being historically motivated but epistemologically ill-founded. Therefore, the integration he advocates is not presented as a new synthesis but as the return to an original, premodern unity. What Menozzi rejects is the idea that scientific interpretation is the only form in which reality can be meaningfully known and interpreted, and that any discourse that exceeds empirical, material reality or does not conform to the strict domain of the hard sciences is worthless. Due to this appreciation of science, Menozzi also appears consistent when prompting new participants in rituals to make an informed choice through a questionnaire utilizing precise medical terminology, while also mitigating Stella Azzurra's responsibility in the case of an accident.

Menozzi resorts as well to science as a repository of data and information that he holds up against the accusation or public perception that ayahuasca is merely a drug, a term that he rejects as inaccurate, while denouncing drug-related policies the world over as inconsistent. He uses scientific information and data to support the idea that ayahuasca is natural and indeed beneficial, especially in the rehabilitation of drug addicts. This creates a symbolically powerful contraposition: in Menozzi's discourse, ayahuasca, falsely claimed to be a drug (in the negative sense) by its critics, is construed as combating drugs themselves.

---

[4] *Catechism of the Catholic Church*, www.vatican.va/archive/ENG0015/__P41.HTM.

Critics of confessional discourses about ayahuasca may point out that a theory like Menozzi's, while incorporating clear scientific language and observations, ultimately overinterprets the interference of ayahuasca with the brain's chemistry as someone's experience of a superior level of consciousness. Menozzi does hint that classical dichotomies – such as mind/brain – are unsatisfactory but he does not fully develop an alternative model. (For extensive interpretations of the states of consciousness induced by entheogens, see Barnard 2014; Cole-Turner 2014; & Hummel 2014.) Santo Daime expert Andrew Dawson, who adopts an ethnographic approach, points out that some beliefs entertained by its practitioners may appear problematic against the backdrop of science. This is the case with supernatural entities that are claimed to be interacting with them during ceremonies (Dawson 2013: 128–31), but also with the therapeutic virtues attributed both to rituals and to ayahuasca itself (Dawson 2013: 100–1, 130). Dawson also observes that the practitioners' perception of modernity is problematic. On the one hand, they distance themselves from the modern world by criticizing materialism, consumerism, and capitalism. On the other hand, they do enjoy the material resources of the modern world, especially those accessible to the middle class; for instance, they regularly fly to Brazil to purchase ayahuasca since its ingredients require climatic conditions that can hardly be replicated outside the Amazon region. This behavior and the linguistic practice that paradoxically join acceptance/usage and refusal are described by Dawson as dislocution (Dawson 2013: 77–9).

Bambini di Satana: History and Beliefs

In 1982, Marco Dimitri (1963–2021) founded in Bologna Bambini di Satana (Satan's Children), which he defined as a "cultural association originating in paganism that considers man and woman as the thinking center of the universe and who can express, through rituals, a self-awareness that harmonizes with the ego" (Dimitri & Lai 2006: 32; for more on this group, see Bigliardi 2021).

Dimitri had no university education. After middle school, he enrolled at a State Technical Industrial Institute, but he dropped out after a year to sign up for a private school from which he graduated with a diploma in telecommunications (Dimitri & Lai 2006: 28; Paolinelli 2007: 44). He was curious about the occult and the paranormal, and, as a teenager, following a UFO sighting, he attended the meetings of the ufologist group Fratellanza Cosmica (Cosmic Brotherhood). As the leader of Bambini di Satana, inspired by British occultist

Aleister Crowley (1875–1947), Dimitri styled himself "La Grande Bestia 666" – The Great Beast 666 (Dimitri 1998) and publicly expressed his ambition to become the reference point for Satanists the world over.

The oath of allegiance that marked one's entry into the group read:

> I swear fidelity to the Work of Satan's Children and to Satan himself, that is, to myself, erect in my nature, in my divine ego. I swear loyalty in my actions following my initiation. By sealing my signature with a drop of blood I proclaim myself Satan. (CESNUR 2021)

The initiation was celebrated by tracing the number 666 with Dimitri's blood on the novice's forehead, who stood naked in front of the congregation.

Bambini di Satana offered various ceremonies, including weddings (for couples, threesomes, and even relatives), baptism rejection, divorces, damnations, and possessions (Introvigne 2010: 399–400). Dimitri and the affiliates performed rituals either in makeshift locations or at a temple in Bologna, the latter being in fact a room in Dimitri's apartment. Furnishings included an altar, effigies of the devil, a wand, a bell, a sword, a chalice, and pentacles, while participants were dressed in cowls. Significantly, however, such paraphernalia were just symbolic and not meant to evoke a personal devil (Dimitri & Lai 2006: 52–3).

Dimitri emphasized that he did not subscribe to a personal and supernatural conception of Satan. National media ignored this fact, however, depicting Dimitri and Bambini di Satana as devil worshippers. Seeking personal attention as well as visibility for the group, Dimitri, ultimately went along with this and was invited to major TV shows.

A "Satanic Panic" led to criminal accusations against Dimitri and a few followers. In January 1996, a girl claimed that Dimitri and other members had sexually assaulted her. Dimitri was incarcerated awaiting trial, and he attempted suicide. It was eventually demonstrated, however, that the claims were unfounded. In a different case six months later, a two-and-a-half-year-old boy started showing anomalous restlessness. His family brought him to a psychologist then, noticing that the therapy bore no significant results, consulted (with the psychologist's approval) an exorcist, who interpreted the child's behavior as the result of Satanic abuse. The exorcist was also spiritually assisting the girl who had made the accusations against Dimitri six months earlier. The exorcist speculated that there was a connection between Dimitri and the young boy, and namely that the child's babysitter was in touch with Bambini di Satana, and had been bringing the child to Satanic rituals in which he had been physically abused. Moreover, the original accuser, confirmed the whole narrative and even stated that she had been participating in such rituals (Beccaria 2006: 62–5). The boy's testimonies were in fact fragmentary and filtered through his relatives and the investigators (Beccaria 2006: 72). Various Catholic figures and agencies such as the GRIS, Gruppo di Ricerca e Informazione sulle Sette (Group for Research and Information on Sects, founded in 1987), influenced trial and media coverage. The GRIS charter was approved by the Italian Episcopal Conference, and the group was housed at the Episcopal See in Bologna. In 2001, it was renamed Gruppo di Ricerca e Informazione Socio-religiosa (Group for Socio-religious Research and Information) (Beccaria 2006: 102). GRIS was consulted both by the boy's mother and by the Carabinieri in charge of the investigations (Beccaria 2006: 104).

The prosecutor suggested that for a Satanist, harming an innocent child was tantamount to harming God (Beccaria 2006: 106). Dimitri responded that he didn't believe either in God or in the devil, adding that children did not even qualify as Catholic, and, being still areligious, they rather were "Satan's children" (Beccaria 2006: 78; Dimitri & Lai 2006: 87). Accusations included notable inconsistencies, such as the theory that Dimitri, upon performing human sacrifices, disposed of the victims' remains in a domestic oven that in fact was neither big nor powerful enough to do so (Beccaria 2006: 84). All charges were ruled to have no merit and Dimitri, having unjustly served thirteen months in jail, was awarded monetary compensation.

While explaining rituals, Dimitri made reference, in particular, to the energy that they mobilized:

> In each and every moment of our life we perform rituals: in order to get to point "B" starting from point "A" we need to follow a certain path. . . . On the energetic plane, things are not different. In order to obtain a specific thing, one needs the help of a specific demon, the demon is conjured with the most appropriate ritual, that is, a set of words and actions that conjure the energy that one wants. Once we have obtained the energetic presence, once we have tuned in with it, we will use the will as a lever to achieve our goal. This is what a ritual is all about, there are neither horrible corpses, nor human bones, nor sacrifices: all this is only based on an iron will. (Dimitri undated)

He also explained:

> By energy I mean matter. Like electricity, magnetism. All forces that are intangible, but that one can feel. Objective, but in the state of energy. I do not mean a spiritual state, because I do not believe in spirits. It's a fascinating dimension, but I do not believe in it. I find New Age trends laughable. They just distort old philosophies. Angels do not exist. And I likewise do not believe in evil eyes, spells, black cats and other superstitions. (qtd. in Paolinelli 2007: 71)

While describing his beliefs, Dimitri would also make statements like the following: "My demon, you left your mark in my DNA and now I have no soul!" (Dimitri & Lai 2006: 15). Or,

> To be the imperfect clones of a perfect God who is power and silence? No, too absurd. The atom possesses a wonderful, logical dynamic. The earth is much older than mankind. It was home to the dinosaurs, it saw glacial eras and billions of preachers whose word was never validated and had to surrender to that demon that is the chaotic motion of the universe. (Dimitri & Lai 2006: 31)

Initially, Dimitri's Satanism oscillated between a Crowleyan esoteric Satanism and one focused on artistic expression. In a phase that followed the judiciary issues, however, he shifted to a markedly rationalist, scientific, and anticlerical version of Satanism. Over those years, Dimitri was professionally active as web designer and web master, and his initiatives as a spiritual leader included an online presence and dissemination of ideas through a constantly updated website. Visitors would be welcomed by the following message:

> RATIONALIST group, not based on a creed. We emphasize that we do NOT believe in spirits, in "god" or the "devil." We only use "Satan" as a synonym of "opposition." From time immemorial, such emancipatory opposition is exerted through SCIENCE, the only tool that can tear apart obscurantism, whatever its origin is. The light that illuminates the darkness is rationality. Our activities: promotion of science as a tool of emancipation. Monitoring religious and/or pseudoscientific abuse.[5]

Except for the name Bambini di Satana in gothic characters – and the very reference to Satan in the message – the website displayed little to no signs related to Satanist symbolism and identity.

Concerning the mission of the association in the later phase, Dimitri included among its goals:

> Dissemination of a mindset receptive towards the idea that humans evolve. Promotion of official science as a tool of evolution in opposition to obscurantism. ... Monitoring pseudoscience-based obscurantism. Dissemination of online material related to all the aforementioned points. ... Dissemination of general-public scientific and cultural information, in defense of secularism, basic human rights, and human self-development. Debunking pseudoscientific hoaxes and theories. (Dimitri 2018, pers. comm.)

In this later phase, which lasted until Dimitri's death in February 2021, he aligned his message with debates, discourses, and campaigns typical of Italian

---

[5] www.bambinidisatana.com. This website is presently offline.

atheist and rationalist associations, including their indictment of pseudoscience. Associations of this kind include CICAP (Comitato Italiano per il Controllo delle Affermazioni sulle Pseudoscienze, Italian Committee for the Investigation of the Claims on Pseudoscience[6]), a skeptics association founded in 1989; and UAAR (Unione degli Atei e degli Agnostici Razionalisti, Union of Rationalist Atheists and Agnostics), founded in 1991. While the former criticizes religious views only in regard to verifiable claims concerning miraculous occurrences, the latter promotes the deconstruction of theology and the denunciation of religion as an institution, criticizing its ordinary practices (for instance, the exclusion of women from Catholic Church hierarchy) and its crimes (such as clerical child abuse). Both associations, however, emphasize the importance of science and rationality.

Dimitri's connections with such associations weren't just linguistic and conceptual. He signed up for UAAR (Dimitri 2011) and, in 2012, he ran in the national elections for the minuscule political party Democrazia Atea, the Atheist Democracy. The party was sometimes erroneously described as led by the famous atheist astrophysicist Margherita Hack (1922–2013), who in fact was just running in the same electoral district as Dimitri. Hack was both the scientific guarantor of CICAP and the honorary president of UAAR.

Bambini di Satana and Science: Commentary

Marco Dimitri's teaching included terms and concepts from science as well as direct, vigorous references to science, such as the capitalized word SCIENCE on his website. Their presence and symbolic significance can be explained in reference to cultural influences as well as to the challenges encountered by Dimitri while he and Bambini di Satana were facing grave charges in court along with intense scrutiny and vilification in the public arena.

No precise scholarly reconstruction of Dimitri's sources has been produced yet. However, one can plausibly assume that, while being fairly conversant with Satanist authors and discourses on the occult, Dimitri also tapped into imagery and linguistic usage current in his time. References to DNA, to dinosaurs, and to the age of the universe resonated with general-public representations of scientific topics over the 1980s and 1990s in Italy and the world over, including cinematic science fiction. DNA, in ordinary Italian language, came to metaphorically signify the essence of something or someone. Additionally, conjuring up electricity and magnetism (whose proper scientific concepts Dimitri had been in all likelihood exposed to in school) was a way to underscore the

---

[6] Initially, the "P" in the acronym stood for *paranormale* – the official reference to *pseudosciences* with a change in the name started being made in 2013.

concrete, nonsupernatural character of Dimitri's Satanism. (More concerning the term energy appears in the next section, under Olav Hammer's analysis.)

In the later phase of Dimitri's Satanism, a priority for him was to strike back against the Catholic Church, which he perceived as the main agency that had inspired accusations and slander against him. In other words, it became imperative for Dimitri not only to reiterate the atheistic character of his position but also to challenge both Catholic beliefs and the Catholic Church as an institution. The language and expressions Dimitri resorted to on the website Bambini di Satana largely reflected those typically used by Italian rationalist associations in their respective official statements and publications. In other words, during the later phase of Dimitri's thought and activism, science was for him a synonym for rationality, and rationality was seen by him as being in stark opposition to (Catholic) religion, which he viewed as superstition.

The conceptualization of science at work in Dimitri's Satanism can be well understood in the light of Jesper Aagaard Petersen's examination of, and reflection over, the role of science in the satanic milieu, although he does not take up Bambini di Satana directly (Petersen 2011). To use Petersen's formula, "modern Satanism is both a secularized esotericism and 'esotericized' secularism" (Petersen 2011: 69). In other words, Petersen observes that Satanists, on the one hand, capitalize on references to science in order to advance a disenchanted and antireligious worldview. On the other hand, Satanists appropriate typical esoteric symbols that are used in the construction of a distinctive identity and profile. Petersen points out the importance of striking a balance between the two: "too much esotericized secularism and you blend into the atheistic, humanistic, and general philosophical critique of religion, losing both the self-religious identity, but also the specific 'edge' provided by the term Satanism itself along the way," he observes, "but too much secularized esotericism and you blend back into the cultic milieu from whence you came" (Petersen 2011: 108–9). Clearly, Dimitri followed similar patterns, and, in fact, in the later phase he began emphasizing science while downplaying occult elements to the point of blending into the atheistic and humanistic milieu.

2 The Scholarly Conversation on New Religious Movements and Science: Historical Studies and Models

The ways in which NRMs conceptualize science has attracted considerable academic attention. A scholar may focus on a specific NRM's discussion of science, be it in the movement's texts or among participants. Reconstructions and commentaries offered in the previous section of this Element are an example of such an approach. Other times, however, scholars are more interested in identifying general historical trends in the conceptualization of science that involve or influence different movements, or in advancing abstract models to describe the ways in which the discussion of science is developed within different NRMs. All such approaches are, of course, connected. Discussions of specific case studies inevitably require historical contextualization since the views on science advocated within a specific NRM undergo appreciable modifications over time, and they can be fully understood only in reference to a historically determined social, political, and cultural context. Additionally, abstract models can only be formulated on the basis of the comparative observation of specific case studies. Finally, the discussion of case studies can benefit from the reference to general typologies.

In the present section, I reconstruct and discuss a few insightful studies by prominent scholars whose scope is broader than the examination of a single NRM. Such scholars either identify historical tendencies or describe typologies or both. They come from various academic backgrounds and adopt different methodologies or conceptualizations of science. Nevertheless, they can be regarded as engaged in a conversation since most of the authors explicitly refer to, and directly cite, each other as significant predecessors or sources of inspiration. Whenever possible, I also touch upon how these contributions shed light on the case studies observed in Section 1, thus bridging the Element's two parts.

Bainbridge: Science as Challenge and Opportunity for New Religious Movements

In a seminal essay titled "New Religions, Science and Secularization," sociologist William Sims Bainbridge observes that, notwithstanding the existence of extensive literature on NRMs, investigating how the advancement of science affects such movements is still a desideratum, and any such attempt must be "exploratory, even experimental" (Bainbridge 1993: 277). In his essay, Bainbridge reflects on how science and religion generally compare and interact. Additionally, he explores how the conception of science conveyed by contemporary scientists who also write for the lay public can impact religious discourses. Finally, he advances suggestions as to future developments of such discourses.

The skepticism of science, points out Bainbridge, seems irreconcilable with faith. Science, therefore, contributes to the erosion of religion in the context of contemporary secularization. A few scholars, notes Bainbridge, would think that, at best, religion and science could arrive at a truce. He suggests, however, that the shrinking of old religions may in fact leave space for new religions that could "achieve a mutually supportive relationship with science." He adds that science even has the potential "to spawn new religions" (Bainbridge 1993: 278).

Bainbridge observes that science and technology haven't solved all the existential problems in which religion traditionally had a say (Bainbridge 1993: 279). Only a few scientists concern themselves with "big issues." Traditionally, science has been imbued with, and has thus conveyed, empiricism – the idea that only the explanations that make reference to visible and measurable causes are valid. Moreover, such causes have been conceived mechanistically and deterministically. However, scientists have developed a new vision according to which natural processes result from a combination of chance and necessity, with a prevalence of the former. Bainbridge suggests that the lay public is still processing this vision, and that it can be perceived as a challenge to the concept of a loving deity who created the universe for humanity (Bainbridge 1993: 280–1).

Bainbridge remarks that systems of belief inspired by, or drawing upon, or cloaked in the scientific terminology of their times, including religious doctrines, are at least as old as Mesmerism – the theory, advanced by the German physician Franz Anton Mesmer (1734–1815). According to Mesmerism, organisms are permeated by animal magnetism, an invisible force whose manipulation has therapeutic potential. Bainbridge also observes that science reaches large audiences through science fiction, which often incorporates references to religions (including fictional ones) as well as to supernatural phenomena. One example he gives is the *Star Wars* saga, with its reference to the Jedi religion (Bainbridge 1993: 282).

As examples of contemporary doctrines that attempt to incorporate a scientific worldview, Bainbridge briefly discusses Transcendental Meditation, Scientology, and the Committee for the Future. Transcendental Meditation, or TM, is a form of meditation that promises the achievement of a superior state of consciousness, as well as psychophysical benefits. It was elaborated by Maharishi Mahesh Yogi (1918–2008) drawing upon Hindu practices, and its popularity peaked between the 1960s and the 1970s. Notably, Maharishi Mahesh Yogi had a degree in physics. The Committee for the Future was an organization of the mid- to late 1970s, originating in, and sustained by, the ideas of the futurist Barbara Marx (1930–2019). It promoted technological development, including space exploration and planetary colonization. Bainbridge explains that all such movements have an uneasy relation with science since they include claims that contradict science, and that the freedom of inquiry that characterizes science can threaten their appeal to authority (Bainbridge 1993: 282).

Bainbridge notes the many instances in which Scientology seems to appropriate the legitimacy of science. He mentions that L. Ron Hubbard was offering titles such as BScN (Bachelor of Scientology) and DScN (Doctor of Scientology), that Scientology doctrines refer to quantification schemes, that its language resorts to scientific-sounding terms, and that the E-Meter, an electronic device, plays an important role in the practice. On the other hand, he points out that Scientologists regard history as obsolete, that Hubbard blamed scientists for the invention of the atomic bomb, and that he opposed scientific materialism. Finally, Bainbridge also comments that the preservation of Tech is at odds with scientific research and therefore stands in the way of any form of collaboration between Scientology and science (Bainbridge 1993: 284).

Finally, in order to explore how NRMs may conceptualize science, Bainbridge engages in a creative exercise imagining the establishment, emergence, expansion, and evolution of the Experimentalist Church, including reference to texts published by its founder in the 2000s. Bainbridge describes him as an electronics engineer who avidly read science fiction. He advanced a "new science" that he later transformed into a church, promising to its members a form of immortality to be achieved through the creation, from DNA samples, of individuals who would be given those very members' memories and personalities and who would establish colonies on planets capable of sustaining life (Bainbridge 1993: 286–9).

Hanegraaff: The New Age and Its "High Regard for Modern Science"

Historian of culture and religion Wouter J. Hanegraaff's *New Age Religion and Western Culture* is a voluminous study of the New Age movement – a manifold, protean, and thus elusive movement that emerged in the second half of the 1970s. It fully blossomed in the 1980s and was still in existence at the time in which Hanegraaff published his monograph (cf. Hanegraaff 1998 [1996]: 12).[7]

The New Age phenomenon was produced, represented, and diffused by an expansive, informal network of authors and practitioners who shared, and variously interpreted, the idea that the world and humanity were entering a new epoch of radical changes concurrently with the coming of a new astrological era. New Age proponents saw themselves as promoting a worldview in opposition to dominant ideas and values that marked the previous two centuries. Hanegraaff's monograph covers a tremendous amount of primary and

---

[7] Wouter J. Hanegraaff published his monograph *New Age Religion and Western Culture*, originally, in 1996 (with Brill). The volume that I have referred to in this Element was published by SUNY Press in 1998.

secondary literature that he examines in great detail and thoroughly discusses. It is important to mention Hanegraaff's identification of various ways in which New Age authors conceptualize science, considering their more or less direct influence on multiple NRMs.

A salient aspect of the New Age movement was the proliferation of perspectives and practices related to healing. New Age representatives regarded Western medicine as only concerned with the biophysical aspects of pathology, and therefore as flawed and limited. In contrast to this approach, they developed and offered a vast array of techniques aimed at improving the social, psychological, and spiritual condition of human beings, convinced as they were that addressing these aspects would bring about the enhancement of physical health as well.

In other words, New Age views fiercely criticize ordinary medicine as well as reject a strong dichotomy between physical and spiritual. Often invoking ancient or traditional medicine, New Age healing is presented as more holistic than simple curing (Hanegraaff 1998 [1996]: 42–3). Additionally, such a perspective usually conjures up the idea that health is a natural condition that can be achieved by respecting nature, rather than an unnatural one that should be artificially obtained by fighting against it (Hanegraaff 1998 [1996]: 46–7). New Age authors tend to prescribe general changes in one's lifestyle and psyche rather than localized, pharmaceutical therapies, and regard themselves as engaged in contrasting materialism and mechanicism, for whose introduction they blame thinkers and scientists such as René Descartes (1596–1650) and Isaac Newton (1643–1727) (Hanegraaff 1998 [1996]: 51–4). Among New Age healing approaches Hanegraaff lists acupuncture, chiropractic, homeopathy, as well healing by crystals, by metal, and by music (Hanegraaff 1998 [1996]: 54–5).

Hanegraaff identifies "high regard for modern science" as an important characteristic of the New Age. This may sound paradoxical given the movement's countercultural thrust. Hanegraaff, however, is careful to specify that New Agers in fact capitalize on recent scientific developments to lend legitimacy to their spiritual views, while at the same time construct such developments as clashing with an "old" science that they describe as mistakenly reductionist and materialist, and consider to be declining (Hanegraaff 1998 [1996]: 62).

Some proponents of the New Age, such as the physicist David Bohm (1917–92) and the chemist Ilya Prigogine (1917–2003) were practicing scientists, while other ones like Fritjof Capra (b. 1939) and Rupert Sheldrake (b. 1942) started off as scientists – physicist and biologist, respectively – but moved on to developing careers as lecturers. In all cases, the possession of scientific credentials lent those figures authority (Hanegraaff 1998 [1996]: 63).

Hanegraaff also points out that the worldviews proposed by such authors stand in contrast with the popularization of science produced and propagated by scientists who wrote for the general public, like Stephen Hawking (1942–2018). Such authors suggest, more or less overtly, that science-informed cosmology can, and should, replace any religious or metaphysical theory. In contrast, New Age authors use science to buttress and promote a unified vision of the cosmos that includes a divine element. In other words, they add an interpretive element to scientific findings and theories (Hanegraaff 1998 [1996]: 63–4). According to Hanegraaff, therefore, what the New Age advances is a religious philosophy of nature rather than science (Hanegraaff 1998 [1996]: 64–5).

Hanegraaff cautions, however, that anyone who sets out to find an alternative to the dichotomy of mind and matter and is inspired by science may end up defending monistic materialism. New Age proponents abhor the latter. As a result, they inevitably have to promote either the idea that science should encompass spiritual realities or the idea that science confirms spiritual realities. Critics, however, object that the former "leads to bad science, and the latter to bad spirituality," while defenders reply that traditional views on science and spirituality are too limited and should be rethought so as to unify the two domains and bring them to a new level (Hanegraaff 1998 [1996]: 172).

Hanegraaff also points to another interesting phenomenon: while the philosophies of nature advanced within the New Age occasionally include reference to testable hypotheses, they are in fact appreciated by their followers because of their perceived beauty and profundity, that is, their capacity to make sense of experience. Critics often attack New Age beliefs while treating them as science, but fail to convince its proponents who, in their turn, phrase responses in a language that incorporates science but fails to convince those very critics. Hanegraaff argues that, as long as such a battle of worldviews is fought in the arena of science, and rationality is philosophically invoked as having supreme authority over truth, there is no hope that any of the parties involved will ever convince the other one (Hanegraaff 1998 [1996]: 66–7).

The conceptualization of bodily and spiritual health typical of the New Age presents significant analogies with the case studies examined in Section 1, especially with those of Dianetics and Falun Gong. It is also reflected in Santo Daime beliefs as interpreted by Menozzi. Hanegraaff acutely captures the way in which these NRMs have been challenged by rationalist, skeptical, and empiricist critics. In addition, Andreas Grünschloß has shown how Scientology fits into the New Age, and explained how they both were influenced by Theosophy (Grünschloß 2009). New Age's influence over Falun Gong seems less clear, however. Penny writes that "Li Hongzhi refers extensively (*though often silently*) to ideas and books that first came into China in the 1980s, notably works of the Western New Age" (Penny 2012: 29; emphasis added; cf. also 109 & 204). However, Susan E. Ackerman, discussing the movement's diffusion in Malaysia, observes that Falun Gong "entered Malaysia in the mid-1990s as a New Age spiritual movement for the mind-and-body development market" and "[it] reflects the widespread practice of New Age groups, styling itself as a spiritual movement rather than a religion" (Ackerman 2005: 496–7).

At least one representative of the New Age discussed by Hanegraaff, Michael Harner (1929–2018), promoted shamanism as a method of healing after having experienced ayahuasca (Hanegraaff 1998 [1996]: 59). While Menozzi distances himself from what he regards as New Age's superficiality in the conceptualiza-tion of shamanism (Menozzi 2013 [2007]: 100 n. 24), he also demonstrates his awareness that the New Age promotes a new religious consciousness (Menozzi 2013 [2007]: 16–7). The way in which he discusses and criticizes mainstream rationalism, materialism, and dichotomies such as bodily/spiritual, while also boosting a "new unification" harking back to shamanism, displays a profound affinity with New Age views.

Hammer: Scientism and Science as "Significant Other"

Historian of religion Olav Hammer's monograph *Claiming Knowledge: Strategies of Epistemology from Theosophy to the New Age* (2004) draws upon Hanegraaff's work. It covers Theosophy and its ramifications as well as multiple New Age authors. Hammer conducts both a historical reconstruction of such movements and authors, and an analysis of the discursive strategies they resorted to as they attempted to define their religious or spiritual position vis-à-vis science.

Hammer sees religion in the post-Enlightenment period as engaged in a struggle with the scientific worldview, perceived as quintessentially represent-ing rationality and knowledge. In this context, according to Hammer, an important mode of legitimation adopted by religious authors is the scientistic one. The use of such an adjective may create confusion with the philosophical notion of scientism – the idea that science is the only field in which solid and worthwhile knowledge can be achieved, a position often embraced by those adopting an antireligious worldview. What Hammer means by scientistic, however, is that religious agents "take the line that scientific inquiry – provided it is interpreted correctly – serves to prove the validity of the religious point of view" (Hammer 2004 [2001]: 203).[8]

---

[8] Hammer interprets what he calls scientism by drawing upon concepts and theories advanced in the social sciences, most notably by Max Weber (1864–1920).

Hammer observes that in the esoteric tradition, science plays the role of a "significant Other" that the authors in such a tradition both distinguish from the teaching they offer and merge with it; additionally, science is used by them in two basic, intertwined ways. First, the representatives of esotericism pin down some elements of science as identifying science as a whole. Second, after reducing science to such select elements, the representatives of esotericism judge science normatively, that is, they formulate an evaluation of it (Hammer 2004 [2001]: 203). In this evaluation of science, esoteric authors are usually ambivalent: they both reject science, for a variety of reasons, and they positively invoke certain pieces of science to construct and buttress their own religious discourse (Hammer 2004 [2001]: 204). Hammer uses the expression creolization to refer to the blending of faith and science and points out the "double construction," "dual nature," and "ambivalent view" inherent in the process of creolization.

One variety of scientism identified by Hammer is represented by nineteenth-century parapsychologists interested in the investigation of life after death, and the interaction of the spirits of the deceased with the world of the living. Hammer points out that parapsychology emulated mainstream science, for instance, with the creation of peer-reviewed journals, and through avowed allegiance to rationalist ideals of the time (Hammer 2004 [2001]: 217).

However, it is Theosophy, created by Helena Petrovna Blavatsky (1831–91) and her circle, that Hammer regards as "an apogee of nineteenth century scientism" (Hammer 2004 [2001]: 218). Born in Yekaterinoslav in the Russian Empire (currently Dnipro in Ukraine), the autodidact, psychic, and world traveler Blavatsky cofounded the Theosophical Society in 1875 in New York. She advanced her views through multiple publications, including the monumental, and convoluted, *Isis Unveiled* (1877) and *The Secret Doctrine* (1888). In a nutshell, Blavatsky elaborated on a number of esoteric themes. She promoted the revival of what she presented as ancient wisdom, a complex cosmogony and cosmology according to which everything proceeds from an impersonal Divine Principle that had been known by, and passed on, ancient sages.

On the one hand, Blavatsky attacked conventional scientists as narrow-minded and materialistic. She also attempted to discredit mainstream scientists by pointing out their discord in certain matters (Hammer 2004 [2001]: 263–4). On the other hand, she invoked science to legitimize her own doctrines: this was done by appropriating scientific notions or narratives and by claiming for her own discourse a scientific status.[9] For Blavatsky, Theosophy qualified as a higher form of science. Hammer points out that, in so doing, Theosophy

---

[9] One example is Lemuria, a land bridge connecting Madagascar and India. The idea was originally raised in nineteenth-century zoological discussions to explain the presence of lemurs in both countries. Theosophists embraced and elaborated upon the theory to support their belief in

furnished the Esoteric Tradition with a discourse on science that has been replicated countless times since then. Each spokesperson argues for his or her own conception of the world as compatible with contemporary science, but also as a body of knowledge that transcends the unnecessary or artificial limitations imposed by materialism. (Hammer 2004 [2001]: 223)

Hammer elaborates in particular on the Austrian esotericist Rudolf Steiner's (1861–1925) criticism of materialism (Hammer 2004 [2001]: 225). Additionally, Theosophical and New Age authors embed their respective interpretations of science, as well as the presentation of their own doctrines, in what Hammer describes as a "U-shaped time-line" – the idea is that modern science is negative, but a new, superior science is underway that in fact points toward ancient wisdom (Hammer 2004 [2001]: 233).

Other manifestations of scientism discussed by Hammer are worth mentioning: they include the techniques used by some of the new religions examined in the previous section; the use of academic endorsements to an author's work or that very author sporting academic titles, including doctorates in fields that are not directly relevant to their discourse (Hammer 2004 [2001]: 236); and the adoption of scientific vocabulary, including terms such as energy, frequency, vibration, dimension, quantum, and the term science itself (Hammer 2004 [2001]: 236–9). Hammer acknowledges, however, that most of such usages are quite old, so it is difficult to pinpoint an exact moment in which they started being used metaphorically (Hammer 2004 [2001]: 237). He underscores as well that such a strategy is widely used (Hammer 2004 [2001]: 239). Mainstream science and parascience are mimicked in the use of journals as platforms, and the utilization of paratechnology, such as "brain tuners" that allegedly improve one's meditative powers (Hammer 2004 [2001]: 239–43). Often, the spokespersons for alternative spiritual or religious views handle opposition from skeptic associations or scientific experts by way of what Hammer calls "mirror-image response," that is, calling themselves the true skeptics who operate in the interest of the general public deceived by the establishment (Hammer 2004 [2001]: 250–3). One may add that the very existence of a dispute between the representatives of science and rationalism and those of an alternative worldview may create the impression that both contenders are representing competing views, but equally academic or scientific ones. Extensive use of footnotes and references, along with other scholarly apparatus also gives the appearance of a scientific approach in confessional texts (Hammer 2004 [2001]: 254).

---

a continent that existed in the ancestral past and was seat of a great civilization (Santucci 2008: 61 n. 85).

Hammer calls one frequently used technique synonymization, which is the claim that certain beings or entities elaborated on in esotericist discourse are nothing else but beings or entities talked about in science (Hammer 2004 [2001]: 266). Finally, Hammer points out that the fusion between religion/ spirituality and science can also be obtained visually, associating images that conjure up, respectively, religious and scientific concepts or figures (Hammer 2004 [2001]: 291).

In sum, Hammer considers scientism as a reflection of an overall religious and spiritual response to the disenchantment of the world brought about by Enlightenment and post-Enlightenment science. In other words, given that science is so powerful and useful (in practical terms) but cannot answer questions of goals, meaning, and purpose, a solution that religion can opt for is to reenchant science itself, that is, to propose a spiritualized science. Another option is to suggest and claim the return to a primeval, more ancient, genuine, and comprehensive form of science (Hammer 2004 [2001]: 321–3). In this regard, Hammer sees analogies between esotericism and Romanticism (Hammer 2004 [2001]: 324–30).

Rothstein: Religion–Science Syncretism and Science as Cognitive Counterweight

In the essay "Science and Religion in the New Religions," historian of religion Mikael Rothstein elaborates on the reasons and the ways in which NRMs conceptualize science and suggests an interpretation of the function of such a conceptualization from a cognitive perspective (Rothstein 2008). What is interesting about his approach is that Rothstein, on the one hand, updates and extends the kind of work that the other scholars so far discussed have offered, reflecting on the science–religion relation and blending historical and discursive analysis. On the other hand, he also proposes adopting the angle of the cognitive sciences, thus enriching and extending the conversation on (new) religions and science by having yet another academic discipline contribute to it.

For starters, Rothstein observes that most people probably use both science and religion to understand the world and balance them according to specific psychological and sociological contexts (Rothstein 2008: 100). He specifies, however, that science is understood within NRMs through a popular, nonexpert perspective. Science thus perceived is unlikely to "live up to ordinary scientific standards," and whenever religion and science are reconciled, it's actually the former that gets the upper hand, while the latter "is largely substituted by a mythological rendering" (Rothstein 2008: 101).

Rothstein argues that in the industrialized world

> science has become fundamental to virtually all walks of life, and it seems
> almost impossible to imagine new religions that do not engage in some kind
> of discussion of interaction with science and technology. . . . No religion of
> the modern world will successfully be able to claim authority without some
> kind of scientific legitimization. (Rothstein 2008: 102)

He contrasts the contemporary situation with that of the seventeenth century, when nascent science had to justify itself in reference to the beliefs held by the religious establishment (Rothstein 2008: 102).

Rothstein invokes sociologist Roy Wallis's famous categorization of NRMs into "world affirming," "world accommodating," and "world rejecting." To put it briefly, while positioning themselves in regard to surrounding society, some NRMs promise to their affiliates a form of spiritual improvement that represents an advantage within ordinary world dynamics (world affirming); other ones define the world as a separate and independent sphere from the spiritual one (world accommodating); yet other NRMs regard the world as corrupted or decadent and in need of change (world rejecting) (Wallis 1984). Similarly, according to Rothstein, some NRMs may affirm or accommodate science in order to obtain societal recognition while other ones may reject science, "seek[ing] to occupy another sociological position" (Rothstein 2008: 107). He suggests, however, that even disregarding science *is* a way of considering science. Drawing upon Hammer's ideas, Rothstein points out that in the contemporary world the mere rejection of science or the simple statement of revelation's priority over science does not pay off (Rothstein 2008: 111). Consequently, NRMs will tend to affirm science, although, as we have already observed, not necessarily in a way that would be universally subscribed to by scientists.

Any encounter of religion and science is a form of syncretism, that is, the merging of two systems; such an alliance, however, is only sought by religion (Rothstein 2008: 108). In his interpretation, merging with science is not just "a matter of missionary strategy" on behalf of religious authors. "In a more general sense," he writes, "science meets religion because they are brought together by creative religious minds" (Rothstein 2008: 109). Not unlike Hammer, Rothstein suggests that scientism (according to Hammer's definition of the term) is a discursive strategy aimed at having religious discourse benefit both from religion and from science, while overall gaining in legitimacy. Leaders and representatives of NRMs, he emphasizes, avoid positing religion and science as completely distinct. Absolute separation can easily be challenged, for instance, by pointing to the explanations that science offers in areas that are relevant to religion, such as cosmology.

NRMs also capitalize on the appeal of rationality represented by science (Rothstein 2008: 111–4).

Of the movements discussed in the previous section, Rothstein touches upon the Raëlians, Satanists, and Scientology. He mentions the Raëlian Movement as relying on "mythological science – a science fiction – even if inspired by earthly, mundane science in a great many ways" (Rothstein 2008: 105). Rothstein describes Satanists as appropriating science in an antitheological vein, adding that "this perspective, however, remains rare and typical only for ideological or semireligious groups that do not entertain notions of the super-natural" (Rothstein 2008: 106). Scientology, he observes, invokes science in its very name, and considers itself scientific both because it can be somehow verified and because it originates from research rather than revelation. He points out that Scientology was born at a time in which science and technology were very influential. "To some extent," he writes, "Scientology actually grew out of science or at least a scientific ambition" (Rothstein 2008: 110). He also notes, however, the conflict that Hubbard had with the scientific community, adding:

> It is possible, therefore, that Scientology, as a soteriological religious system, owes its existence partly to this conflict with the conventional scientific community that made it impossible for Hubbard to continue as he originally intended. In fact, it may be the poor scientific standard of the alleged science of *dianetics* that led Hubbard to modify his system into a religion. (Rothstein 2008: 110–1; original emphasis)

In addition to elaborating on Hammer's suggestions, Rothstein draws upon Bainbridge's views, as well as on ideas advanced by James R. Lewis. However, he also takes concepts from cognitive anthropologist and evolution-ary biologist Pascal Boyer, in order to advance a third perspective, which Rothstein labels "a psychological theory" (Rothstein 2008: 114).

Boyer observes that religions incorporate counterintuitive elements, that is, narratives and doctrines that challenge the ordinary understanding of the world, a case in point being miraculous or supernatural narratives. On the one hand, such elements catch one's attention, and help in memorizing myths and sacred narratives. On the other hand, they cannot be overly prevalent, lest they wreck the overall credibility of the very religion they are embedded in. Therefore, counterintuitive narratives and concepts demand to be counterbalanced by mundane ones (Rothstein 2008: 114).

In this framework, Rothstein proposes that NRMs' references to science be interpreted as playing the role of counterweight to counterintuitive elements. To be sure, he is aware that actual science can in fact be unintelligible, and even seem miraculous to the nonexpert. Nevertheless, he remarks that science is popularly associated with a "naturalistic, rationalist and nonsupernatural" understanding of the world, which creates a balance in regard to the outlandish elements of the very religious narratives and doctrines in which such references are encapsulated (Rothstein 2008: 115).

Finally, Rothstein sees the fact that NRMs prove able to sacralize science, and use it to strengthen their legitimacy as "perhaps the most important aspect of the science–religion problem pertaining to the new religions" and "a signifi-cant feature of the dynamics of the so-called postmodern culture" (Rothstein 2008: 116).

Zeller: Three Case Studies, a Threefold Typology, and Two Predictors

Religion scholar Benjamin E. Zeller published *Prophets and Protons: New Religious Movements and Science in Late Twentieth-Century America*, an important monograph that, not unlike Hammer's study, complements a historical exploration with the elaboration of an abstract model that describes how NRMs conceptualize science (Zeller 2010). He focuses on three cases: the Unification Church, the International Society for Krishna Consciousness (ISKCON), and Heaven's Gate. The first movement originated in Korea with Sun Myung Moon (1920–2012), who founded it in 1954, and then it spread to Japan, the United States, and Europe (for a history of the Unification Movement, see Mickler 2023). ISKCON, also known as Hare Krishna, was founded in New York in 1966 by Swami A. C. Bhaktivedanta Prabhupada (1896–1977) and spread worldwide (for a history of ISKCON, see Burt 2023). Heaven's Gate was founded in 1974 in the United States by Bonnie Nettles (1927–85) and Marshall Applewhite (1931–97) and attracted, at its apex, several hundred followers; it remains known for the collective suicide committed in 1997 by Applewhite and thirty-eight active members (for a history of Heaven's Gate, see Zeller 2014).

Zeller points out that in the early 1970s, concomitantly with major scientific development in genetics, physics, and computer science, "science had become so big, powerful, and important that all religions had to respond to it" and therefore "new religions reacted to science with a clarity and alacrity that more established religions could not" (Zeller 2010: 2). In other words, science operated as a "powerful symbol" (Zeller 2010: 17). Each one of the movements examined, however, responded to science differently.

The Unification Church had a twofold approach to religion and science. It both constructed them as separate spheres and, at the same time, also aimed at directing science, by dictating its ethics, methods, and goals. The concrete manifestation of this aspiration was a series of international conferences on the unity of the sciences subsidized by the Church (twenty-two between 1972 and 2000, and one in 2017) that attracted prominent scientists including Nobel laureates. The Church's founder and leader Sun Myung Moon, who was trained in electrical engineering, regarded religion as access to metaphysical truths that dictated a unification on multiple levels. First, scientific fields had to be unified so as to avoid a fragmentary approach to reality, thus living up to science's mandate to remove ignorance of the material world. Second, religion and science had to be unified by having the first sponsor, patronize, and guide the latter, providing it with ethical principles dictated by that divine dimension that science itself does not study directly, and without which it may become destructive – as demonstrated by environmental catastrophes. Third, all religions had to be unified. Additionally, Unificationism was conceptualized as a rational religion, appealing to the "cognitive abilities [of its followers] rather than to emotions or faith" (Zeller 2010: 43), thus rejecting, for instance, miracles and wonders.

ISKCON aspired to replace science through its own scientific–religious system that drew upon Hindu tradition. Its founder was convinced that God could be known scientifically, through a process that could be taught to others. But he also believed that Western science had failed, having turned immoral and arrogant. Mainstream science had to give way to religion, which Swami Prabhupada explicitly presented as a science that he explained in a language incorporating scientific terminology. The swami had left India for the United States in 1965, but quickly found a receptive audience among hippie counterculture. His rejection, indeed his denigration – including strong, disparaging language – of Western science and scientists can be understood as an expression of anticolonialist sentiments and goals. Zeller adds, however, that such distrust toward Western science also appealed to, and was strengthened by, the critical attitude toward science and authority that Prabhupada found in the US counterculture (Zeller 2010: 88–9).

The founders of Heaven's Gate, through a series of teachings that they kept enriching and revising over two decades, offered a transition from the human level to a next level (but still physical) to be achieved through a special, exacting lifestyle that included fasting and sexual abstinence. Zeller emphasizes that initially Heaven's Gate offered a biological transition to the next level, but Applewhite later reconceptualized such transition as the dropping of human "vehicles" on behalf of consciousness that would transfer into the next level (Zeller 2010: 146–7). In the last formulation, the transition was going to be mediated through space travel by extraterrestrial beings that were described as managing the universe and were believed to be coming in a spacecraft trailing the Hale–Bopp comet. Such extraterrestrials would allow select, deserving humans to join their life, immune from human limitations and characterized by peace, rationality, and group mindedness. The comet appeared in 1996 but became spectacularly visible in the early months of 1997, an occurrence followed by Heaven's Gate collective suicide.

Applewhite and Nettles were explicit about the fact that the salvific process they were offering was chemical and biological as opposed to spiritual, symbolic, and supernatural (Zeller 2010: 125; cf. also 127). Zeller specifies that, in their usage of terminology identifiable as scientific, they "represented a far wider American religious mind-set" typical of the New Age (Zeller 2010: 128).

Heaven's Gate posited science as synonymous with "truth, rationalism, reasonability and the reliance on evidence" and religion as characterized by "falsehood, emotionalism, no sensibility, and reliance on faith" (Zeller 2010: 118). The system of Heaven's Gate was therefore presented as belonging to the former, while religion was being dismissed. Nevertheless, points out Zeller, Heaven's Gate fully functioned as a religion. Additionally, Applewhite and other "students," as members called themselves, also associated science with empiricism and atheism, which they rejected (Zeller 2010: 154). One member of Heaven's Gate who would eventually commit suicide used the jargon of *Star Trek*, calling the group an "away team," just as the television series defined crew members who visited a planet while leaving their spaceship (Zeller 2010: 161).

Zeller uses the three movements to propose a threefold typology that indicates how religion understands science and positions itself in its regard. First, religion may want to guide science toward religiously established goals. Second, religion may aim at replacing mainstream science with an alternative scientific system. Third, the religious system may attempt to absorb the methodology of science. The three options respond to historical and social circumstances – the rapid growth of science in postwar United States and its different perceptions on behalf of mainstream culture, subcultures, and countercultures. NRMs responded to science in much more radical ways than America's major religions, given the absence of strong theological or institutional constraints on their respective theologies (Zeller 2010: 163–4).

Zeller also offers an explanation regarding the variables that may have led the movements at stake to opt for their respective conceptualizations of science. Notably, such variables can also act as predictors for the understanding of, and position on, science assumed by other movements.

Both ISKCON and the Unification Church were born in a colonial context and regarded science as powerfully linked with the West. Swami Prabhupada, however, rejected Western culture wholesale – and so he did with science. Rev. Moon, having experienced scientific modernization mediated by the Japanese rather than by Western colonizers, regarded it as a force – just one that needed guidance. Heaven's Gate, with no colonial background, embraced science unconditionally (Zeller 2010: 166).

A second predictor is a religion's position regarding mind and body. Drawing upon traditionally Hindu ideas, including the conceptualization of the world as an illusion, ISKCON devalues the physical side of human beings. Consequently, science is belittled, since it is perceived as imperfect knowledge of an imperfect dimension. Throughout the different formulations of its doctrines, Heaven's Gate adopted a strong materialist outlook that combined well with the movement's acceptance of science. In between these two viewpoints, one finds that Unificationism opted for a balanced dualism, according to which human beings exist both as body and brain, and mind and soul. This led adherents to value both scientific and spiritual knowledge (Zeller 2010: 167–8).

A brief look at the NRMs explored in Section 1 through the lens of Zeller's typology confirms its insightfulness. None of the movements at stake were born in a colonial context in which science was strongly associated with ideas of usurpation and prevarication. Correspondingly, none of them incorporate a strong rejection of science or an attempt to replace it wholesale. To be sure, Scientology, Falun Gong, and Santo Daime/Stella Azzurra emerged in different cultural milieus. Nevertheless, each milieu included both appreciation of science and mistrust toward it, if in different proportions. Even Li Hongzhi, while being influenced by Communist ideological optimism about science and technology, could not ignore ecological concerns typical of the 1980s and 1990s, as indicated by his mention of the hole in the ozone layer. Similar observations are true for the Raëlians and Bambini di Satana, which both opted to vigorously emphasize the importance of science in order to mark their strong distinction from traditional religions. In this respect, Raëlians and Satanists are analogous to Heaven's Gate. Additionally, none of the NRMs observed in Section 1 emphasize the import-ance of the spiritual level to the total detriment of the bodily dimension. Scientology, Falun Gong, and Santo Daime/Stella Azzurra, while aiming at spiritual development, also promise physical benefits along the way. As a result, they all represent moderate, dualistic positions not too distant from the position of the Unification Church as Zeller describes it. The Raëlian Movement and Bambini di Satana are neatly materialist, and, correspondingly, they represent a robust endorsement of science.

Lewis: Religion's Appeal to the Authority of Science – Seven Strategies Used by New Religions

Building upon ideas advanced by Hanegraaff, Hammer, Rothstein, and Zeller, religion scholar James R. Lewis discusses religion's appeal to science as a strategy to enhance the legitimacy of religion in his essay "How Religions Appeal to the Authority of Science" (Lewis 2011). In this work, Lewis draws on his own study of legitimation strategies in new religions (Lewis 2003). In the 2011 work, however, he focuses on strategies that invoke science. Lewis observes that the existence of such strategies may seem strange to some, since one may rather think that religion per se is a form of legitimation (Lewis 2011: 23). He asserts that the term strategy should be taken metaphorically, writing that "religious leaders [do not] necessarily set out to design legitimation strategies in the same way business executives develop marketing strategies or generals develop military strategies" and that a religion's appeal to science "emerge[s] more or less spontaneously out of the ongoing life of the [religious] community" (Lewis 2011: 24–5). He acknowledges as well that "the lines of division between these legitimation strategies are often hazy and overlapping" (Lewis 2011: 25).

An individual who is actively engaged as a scientist, points out Lewis, may regard science as authoritative because of its rationality. The general population, however, may accord prestige to science both because it has come to be regarded quasi-religiously – this, before the emergence of Cold War concerns and the ecological critique of science – and because of the daily perception of technology (and, by implication, of science) as a powerful and effective problem solver (Lewis 2011: 26). According to Lewis, this resulted in the incorporation into religious and spiritual doctrines of typically scientific notions such as that of laws, drawing upon Isaac Newton's (1643–1727) usage of the term (Lewis 2011: 26–7). Some movements regard themselves as scientific in the sense of empirically exploring a certain set of phenomena and coming up with a systematic doctrine thereof (Lewis 2011: 27–8). Other religions and movements draw parallels between science and their worldview (Lewis 2011: 28–9).

Lewis proposes a typology of the ways in which religions make appeals to science. He identifies seven strategies typically used by new religions. First, the terminological/rhetorical strategy is applied when a religious doctrine is labeled as "science" or "scientific," or when it is formulated in scientific-technological terminology, or when traditional religious beliefs and practices are redescribed as scientific. Lewis lists as falling under this strategy the case in which traditional practices (such as astrology) present a "systematic/quantitative" dimension that can be perceived as scientific. The second strategy, which Lewis calls methodological, is closely related to the first one and consists of presenting a religious doctrine as the result of empirical, systematic research (for instance into the soul). The third strategy is the advocacy of a naturalistic worldview in which appeals to natural, rather than supernatural, explanation are employed. A fourth strategy is the emphasis put on academic research on religious practices; in other words, when a religion itself becomes the object of scholarly investigation, it tries to gain legitimation by pointing out that scientists or scholars outside the religion are interested in it. The fifth strategy is the development or incorporation, in a religious doctrine, of alternative science or even fringe science. The sixth strategy is the use of some type of paratechnology, such as the E-Meter in Dianetics/Scientology. Finally, the seventh strategy is to establish academic institutions (schools, academies), or to emphasize that members hold doctorates or boast academic credentials, including ones unrelated to religion. Lewis is careful to specify that this typology is provisional and heuristic, and he reiterates that the categories listed are not "hermetically sealed" (Lewis 2011: 31–3).

Wrapping up his essay, Lewis identifies two more reasons why science is a natural choice for legitimation in a world in which different religious economies compete. First, scientific truths are perceived to be universal. Second, science, even when it is not mobilized to criticize religion, seems a natural competitor to religion itself, given that it addresses questions that traditionally were answered by religion, including fields like cosmology and the definition of human nature (Lewis 2011: 37).

Of the movements we have closely observed in Section 1, Lewis briefly touches upon the Raëlians, Satanism, and Scientology. He mentions the Raëlian Movement as an example of an NRM that subscribes to a naturalistic interpretation of modern science, indeed "the most thoroughly secular of all the UFO religions" (Lewis 2011: 31). Satanism is likewise hinted at by Lewis as being based on a naturalistic worldview (Lewis 2011: 32; see also Petersen 2011). He mentions Scientology as using scientific terminology, mimicking scientific methodology, and resorting to paratechnology (Lewis 2011: 32, 36).

Some of the strategies described by Lewis also appear in Falun Gong: for instance, the incorporation of scientific terminology and of "fringe science" (when Li Hongzhi mentions the trilobite with the "footprint" on it, he is in fact resorting to an old creationist narrative). Santo Daime/Stella Azzurra incorporate scientific terminology and mention scholarly work about the religion. Scientology resorts to even more strategies than Lewis identifies in it. For instance, Hubbard relied upon (alleged/invented) academic titles for himself and members. Moreover, Scientology websites mention renowned scholars' evaluation of Scientology as a bona fide religion (Church of Scientology International 2022b). Finally, Scientology also systematically reformulates the teachings of other religions, claiming Scientology's continuity with older religious traditions that are considered approximations of Hubbard's discoveries and teachings; one notable case is the depiction of Sufism, a form of Islamic mysticism, in official Scientology literature (Bigliardi 2015c).

Von Stuckrad: The Scientification of Religion

In a relatively brief but complex and insightful monograph, cultural historian Kocku von Stuckrad explores how science and religion were attributed different meanings in cultural communication and practice between the end of the nineteenth century and the beginning of the twentieth (von Stuckrad 2015). His perspective on natural science is a moderately constructivist one. While not denying the existence of "a world out there," he contends that scientific practices and procedures "materialize" discourses and such "materializations ... stabilize and legitimize the discursive assumptions that have made them possible" (von Stuckrad 2015: 9). That being said, he mostly uses science in a broad sense, referring to organized, academic knowledge. While not extensively discussing any of the NRMs reconstructed in this Element, von Stuckrad does examine theories and trends that display remarkable intersections and overlaps with NRMs, such as alchemy, astrology, esotericism, Theosophy, Jungian psychology, paganism, and witchcraft.

Von Stuckrad notes that elements from knowledge systems that were discarded by official, academic knowledge in fact survive within forms of accepted knowledge. For example, alchemic concepts were reinterpreted and maintained within Jungian psychology. At the same time, however, academic and secular understandings of religion have an impact on religious discourses, including the very fact that such discourses touch upon science. Von Stuckrad uses the expression "scientification of religion" to signify that the borders between religion and science are constantly negotiated.

Scientification involves both the natural sciences and science broadly meant as scholarly, systematized knowledge. "Emic terms – even those that used to have very strong evaluative connotations – can be turned into etic categories," writes von Stuckrad. "What makes these terms 'etic' is the simple fact that scholars use them; thus, calling something 'etic' is perhaps not more than a rhetorical device to give an emic term scholarly power and blessing." However, there also exists the reverse process, "with so-called etic concepts being turned into emic ones." He concludes that "the very differentiation between emic and etic is constantly negotiated and dependent on power relations" (von Stuckrad 2015: 154). He adds that "the academic and the practitioner form a discourse community in which all actors inform and stimulate one another" (Von Stuckrad 2015: 177). Von Stuckrad thus suggests challenging "overly simplistic binary constructions, not only between religion and science, but also between emic and etic, professional and amateur, academic and vernacular, as well as between center and periphery" (von Stuckrad 2015: ix).

As mentioned above, Lewis observes that some NRMs draw on their own discussion on behalf of academic experts in order to claim legitimacy. I noted that Scientology resorts to citing the work of various scholars to confirm its own religious nature. In this case, one may think that Lewis's typology fits perfectly, since different discursive boundaries can clearly be discerned: the very creators of the religious discourse maintain the distinction between themselves and the experts in order to gain legitimacy from referencing the latter. Von Stuckrad makes a deeper and compelling point, however. Indeed, the moment one steps back and scrutinizes discursive practice, including its history and its potential developments, recognizing or keeping track of the boundaries between emic and etic becomes challenging. Those very scholars cited by Scientology were only able to offer academic reconstructions of Scientology's doctrines by drawing upon its foundational texts and the practitioners' self-understanding collected through ethnographic work. In other words, what began as emic was turned into etic, only to be picked up and reincorporated in emic discourse. I am offering here an emic understanding of that very process, which may well be picked up by Scientologists again, in a potentially infinite game of mirrors.

An example of scientification mentioned by von Stuckrad is

> the positive attribution of religious meaning to the use of ayahuasca and other psychoactive plants [being] discursively stabilized in the genre of academic publication [where] the strict differentiation between emic and etic turns out to be analytically useless. (Von Stuckrad 2015: 155)

This is fully confirmed by the case study of Stella Azzurra. I have observed how Menozzi's monograph on ayahuasca carries a confessional discourse in which academic literature and scientific language are absorbed and mobilized to conceptualize the NRM leader's very understanding of his sacrament. At the same time, Menozzi shows that he is so articulate and competent in entheogens that he wouldn't look out of place on an academic panel on the topic.

All the scholars who contributed to the conversation on NRMs and science as I have reconstructed it in this section have produced "variations" within established fields. In other words, they have embraced one or more methods – historical reconstruction, conceptual and discursive analysis – with the possible exception of Rothstein, who has suggested involving the cognitive sciences. They have advanced views that extended or refined their colleagues' ones. While doing so, they have been keeping within academic boundaries. In other words, all of these scholars have relied, more or less explicitly, on a firm distinction between an etic and an emic perspective, that is, between a scholarly/external viewpoint (the one they represented), and an internal one to the NRMs. What is fascinating and worthwhile about von Stuckrad's contribution is that he effectively challenges the very dichotomy between emic and etic. I shall elaborate on some possible implications of his suggestion in the next section.

3 Engaging with New Religious Movements and Science: Ways Ahead

Conceptualizations of science prominently feature in many NRMs. Science offers plenty of terms that can be used to describe spiritual experiences. Positively equated with rationality, science can be invoked as a legitimizer, but can also be enlisted against the alleged irrationality of other belief systems. Yet when it is deemed deficient or destructive, science can be antagonized. It can also be patronized. Often, multiple such options are simultaneously embraced, with different degrees of emphasis and nuance, within the same NRM. Critics, too, may mobilize science to challenge NRMs, for instance, pointing out that they convey pseudoscientific notions, or that they misleadingly and harmfully compete with science – most notably, medicine – or that they include distortions or oversimplifications of science. Scholars scrutinize and compare NRM discourse on science including founders' texts and members' statements, looking for general trends, and coming up with typologies to describe the ways in which science is used.

There is wide scholarly consensus concerning the importance of considering conceptualizations of science within NRMs' theologies in order to gain a deep comprehension of such movements. It is also generally recognized that this kind of investigation allows one to grasp crucial postmodern cultural dynamics. Science, however perceived, carries enormous symbolic significance, and no theory or theology that aims to make sense of the world and of human existence can avoid tackling it – even neglect of science or its criticism are significant responses.

As part of the process of modern secularization, older religious systems are increasingly marginalized, fragmented, and subject to rational or science-based criticism. In response to the latter challenge, contemporary theologians and other exegetes can reinterpret ancient scriptures, arguing that they are not incompatible with modern science, or, sometimes, that they are supported by scientific research, or even that they encapsulate science. (The third option is particularly well represented within contemporary Islam, with exegetes pointing out that the Qur'an – revealed fourteen centuries ago – contains astonishingly precise scientific notions that were only verified in modern times [Bigliardi 2014].) These approaches, however, may elicit criticism on behalf of coreligionists who regard such positions as far-fetched or unnecessarily obsequious toward science and modernity. In contrast, some NRMs' theology often features extensive, explicit, and direct references to science since their very inception. This represents a significant evolution of what used to be called "religion": new and alternative spiritualities "may prove more hardy and resistant to the disenchanting forces that their antecedents were ill equipped to deal with" (Partridge 2004: 40).

Arguably, the conceptualization of science within NRMs' belief systems is often far from what it is perceived to be science by professional scientific communities. In particular, science's scope and promises are often overstated when they are invoked as a legitimizer or positively discussed within NRMs – consider, for example, the promise of immortality that Raëlians associate with cloning. Science, in other words, is often enchanted. Because science requires considerable skill and education in order to be understood in depth, mythologizing it one way or another is easier than actually grasping and mastering it. Due to its efficiency and complexity, technology inspires magical thinking. To put it with sci-fi writer Arthur C. Clarke's (1917–2008) famous adage: "Any sufficiently advanced technology is indistinguishable from magic" (Clarke 2013 [1973]: 38, fn.). Science's complexity, however, may also explain why it makes for a polemical target – for instance, it is much easier to attack the theory of evolution than to understand its technicalities.

New religious and spiritual movements are born, spread, branch off, and evolve with great frequency, thus making for a nearly inexhaustible subject of study. Correspondingly, analysis of their relation with science is virtually neverending. To this should be added that the very development of science and technology unceasingly creates possibilities and challenges that inevitably impinge on religious discourses. If we set out to study the relation of NRMs and science, we will hardly find ourselves short of research material. That being said, an interesting question is what directions such study may take.

While focusing on novel or unexplored NRMs, researchers may opt, methodologically speaking, for a beaten path. For instance, they may want to determine whether an NRM conforms to, or challenges, extant typologies. It will be interesting to see if the models discussed in this Element will prove able to capture all the ways in which new religious discourses theorize religion and science. Scholars may also want to check whether a new case study warrants the extrapolation of a novel typology, compare such model with other ones, apply it to already investigated NRMs, and so on. Another way to develop the study of NRMs and science while keeping within the boundaries of familiar methodologies is the investigation of whether an NRM's members, in their perceptions of science, fully agree with their respective leaders and scriptures, or how members with advanced educational degrees, possibly including scientific ones, make sense of supernatural or antiscientific ideas. A researcher may also opt for comparative studies of NRMs and science focusing on specific topics. For instance, it would be interesting to assess analogies and differences in the ways in which various NRMs (but also older religions) discuss space exploration, exobiology, evolution, human cloning, AI, vaccines, just to mention a few issues.

Bainbridge briefly develops an interesting example of engagement with NRMs and religion, describing a fictional NRM's conceptualization of science. Creative scholars and students may want to imagine an NRM, instead of waiting for one to appear and dissect it. There may be value in trying to see if it is possible to design an NRM in such a way as to make it a plausible yet unique conceptualization of science, radically different from those that have been observed so far.

Rothstein's idea to interpret scientific references as cognitive stabilizers for unconvincing religious beliefs within a given system is also worth further investigation and discussion. His recommendation to resort to the cognitive sciences may prove enlightening also in order to bridge perceived differences between NRMs and older religions. In other words, when observed from a cognitive perspective, NRMs and other religions may turn out to be more similar than they initially appeared; this may also be true regarding their respective ways of dealing with science.

Other lines of investigation sketched in the scholarly discussions that we have observed, and that seem well worth pursuing or developing, include researching how science and technology are visually conceptualized within NRMs (cf. Hammer 2004 [2001]: 291; Battaglia 2007: 165; Zeller 2011: 106); or how NRMs' conceptualizations of science intersect with literary or cinematic science fiction motifs (cf. Bainbridge 1993: 282). Yet another approach is to investigate how science has been used in court to discuss aspects or practices of NRMs (as with Scientology's E-Meter, or with ayahuasca in Menozzi's case, as reconstructed in this Element).

Another interesting research focus could be the way in which NRMs respond to science-based criticism, such as the debunking produced and popularized by skeptical and rationalist organizations. The role that science-based doubts and objections play for those leaving NRMs – including activists publicly attacking their old religion – may well be worth studying.[10] Additionally, it would be fascinating to apply to the very organizations and authors that produce and

---

[10] During the pandemic, Ex-Jehovah's Witness Harrison Cother (b. 1994) started criticizing his former religion through his *YouTube* channel (www.youtube.com/c/TheTruthHurts/featured). He also resorted to rationalist arguments such as the clash between evolutionary ideas and Jehovah's Witnesses' literalist reading of Genesis.

promote the debunking of pseudoscience, the same scholarly methods used for NRMs. Scrutinizing how they conceptualize religion and science in their respective charters, whether their actual practice is consistent with officially declared intentions, and whether such attitudes are fully grasped and implemented by members would be illuminating (cf. Dyrendal 2011).

Following other threads may even lead to paradigm shifts in the very methods used to research and interpret science and NRMs. For instance, it would be fascinating to explore the consequences of a vigorous philosophical questioning of the anthropology and epistemology underpinning the theoretical frameworks adopted by NRM scholars. As this Element demonstrates, a number of experts agree that science functions as a source of authority and legitimation. To be sure, most of the time this idea seems largely defensible, especially when extensive evidence is available as to the existence of considerable social pressure on a given NRM on behalf of a milieu that is highly appreciative of science, as in the case of Falun Gong and Qi Gong in China. Other NRMs, like Scientology and Santo Daime/Stella Azzurra, even had to face science-based criticism in court. We shouldn't ignore, however, that science-based legitimization isn't always consistently detected through ethnographic work, a case in point being the results initially obtained by Dericquebourg for Scientologists in France.

In other words, one should not overstate the idea that NRM representatives are haunted by the concern of defending their claims, or that NRM leaders invariably design their respective belief systems while having in mind a competition with other views and/or with science. It is not illogical or farfetched to state that NRMs are born and emerge in the context of a war of all against all among belief systems that end up being interiorized by their founders and members. On reflection, however, the actual existence of such interiorization also seems ultimately unverifiable and hardly extrapolatable. At times, one might suspect that science-based legitimization may be elicited by ethnographic work rather than being originally and pervasively present in the practitioners' self-understanding. Even Lewis, one of the scholars who mostly emphasizes the concept of science's authority, also cautions that the idea of a "legitimation strategy" should be taken metaphorically. One may well wonder: if a strategy is only metaphorically conceived, then what is it, exactly? Social scientists, who are overrepresented in new religions studies, tend to craft on their own, and to discuss among themselves, the epistemologies underpinning their respective theoretical frameworks, the discussion of NRMs and science being no exception. It would therefore be interesting to see more conversation on these points among NRM experts and specialists in epistemology and other philosophical branches, such as the philosophy of language.

This Element has focused on the beliefs of NRMs in relation to science, reconstructing scholarly typologies for understanding this dynamic relationship. But such models can well be used to study older religions or their contemporary developments and interpretations. For instance, Lewis and Hammer's 2011 *Handbook of Religion and the Authority of Science* offers discussions in the light of the concept of science's authority, of modern trends within Hinduism, Buddhism, Judaism, Christianity, and Islam. In fact, interesting taxonomies for the relation of science and religion have been advanced by a range of scholars, mainly making reference to major religions and their modern or contemporary theological developments. Such taxonomies may well be applied to NRMs (e.g., Barbour 2000; Stenmark 2004; Peters 2018).

The models discussed in this Element are etic, that is, they are explanations of NRMs advanced by scholars who do not intend to participate in theological, emic discussion, or elaboration among religious leaders and affiliates (at least in the essays analyzed here, for which they adopt a neutral/impersonal style). We have observed, however, that Kocku von Stuckrad effectively demonstrates the high volatility of the emic/etic distinction. Additionally, religion–science models have been proposed that function as both emic and etic. For instance, Ian Graeme Barbour (1923–2013), who is often credited with founding the academic study of religion and science, advanced a fourfold taxonomy – *conflict, independence, dialogue,* and *integration* – useful for describing notable positions in the history of the science–religion relation (Barbour 2000). As a Christian engaged in the debate over science and religion, however, Barbour also took a precise evaluative stance on each category he identified, thus making suggestions that could be (and are) used in theological debates. Barbour's work is a good example of how descriptive and normative perspectives, as well as etic and emic ones, variously overlap. To use von Stuckrad's parlance, Barbour conflated scholar and practitioner. In fact, since Barbour held degrees both in physics and in divinity, the very fields he discussed were merged in his own figure.

How is one to precisely interpret von Stuckrad's challenge to the emic/etic distinction, and other, related ones? Shall scholars strive to retain and implement these differences? Shall the separation of ethnographic and theological conversations be maintained as useful and reassuring devices, if artificial and ultimately weak ones? Alternatively, one may want to fully embrace a blurring of categories that, following von Stuckrad's suggestions, is always and invariably at work, if with different degrees of visibility. NRMs do not currently seem sufficiently developed or socially accepted to have their representatives fully and officially join theological conversations with representatives of academia and of other belief systems. In other words, with a few exceptions, NRM representatives are not recognized as serious interlocutors to be invited to and heard on a footing of equality with representatives of other religions at interfaith or theological debates focused on the theme of science and religion.[11] This need not be the case forever; indeed, lines may already have been crossed or blurred, at least in notable if limited cases such as the discussion of entheogens. Scholars may thus expect that interdisciplinary, theological, and interreligious conversation will be slowly but significantly joined by representatives of at least some NRMs offering discussions from their particular viewpoint. Alternatively, some NRMs, like the Unification Church in the past, may become powerful enough to sponsor, host, and participate in such conversations.

A third scenario is the one in which those in academia decide to acknowledge, develop, or even accelerate the process of dialogue about science. This would require reshuffling extant power relations and setting up inclusive conversations in which religion and science are discussed both by internal and external observers of different fields and belief systems. This would include social and natural scientists, theologians, and NRM members – as well as figures at the intersection of such categories – but even critics of NRMs and of religion in general.

Admittedly, the outcome of such conversations may be chaotic, challenging, and confusing to some. Following one of Hanegraaff's suggestions, we may discover that, at least in some cases, upon setting up a conversation of this kind, one is simply left with a dialogue of the deaf. However, such a decision may even result in the discovery of novel ways of engaging with religion and science both on behalf of different scholars and of NRM representatives. It would be a worthwhile endeavor.

---

[11] For example, Scientologist Eric Roux has published academic works on Scientology, serves on interfaith boards, dialogues with scholars at conferences, and has made inroads into some mainstream interfaith circles (www.uri.org/eric-roux) (Westbrook 2022b, pers. comm.). Here, however, I am referring specifically to debates (including conferences, edited volumes, and so on) on religion and science.

References

Ackerman, S. E. (2005). "Falun Dafa and the New Age Movement in Malaysia: Signs of Health, Symbols of Salvation." *Social Compass*, 52(4): 495–511.

Bainbridge, W. S. (1993). "New Religions, Science and Secularization." *Religion and the Social Order*, 3A: 277–92.

Barbour, I. G. (2000). *When Science Meets Religion. Enemies, Strangers, or Partners?* San Francisco, CA: HarperSanFrancisco.

Barker, E. (2004). "Perspective: What Are We Studying? A Sociological Case for Keeping the '*Nova*'." *Nova Religio*, 8(1): 88–102.

Barnard, G. W. (2014). "Entheogens in a Religious Context: The Case of the Santo Daime Religious Tradition." *Zygon*, 49(3): 666–84.

Battaglia, D. (2007). "Where Do We Find Our Monsters?" In J. Edwards, P. Harvey and P. Wade, eds., *Anthropology and Science: Epistemologies in Practice*. London: Routledge, pp. 153–69.

Beccaria, A. (2006). *Bambini di Satana*. Rome: Stampa Alternativa.

Bigliardi, S. (2014). "What We Talk about When We Talk about *i'jāz*." *Social Epistemology Review and Reply Collective*, 4(1): 38–45. https://social-epis temology.com/2014/12/15/what-we-talk-about-when-we-talk-about-i%CA%BFjaz-stefano-bigliardi/.

Bigliardi, S. (2015a). "New Religious Movements and Science: Raël's Progressive Patronizing Parasitism." *Zygon*, 50(1): 64–83.

Bigliardi, S. (2015b). "Il fascino sfacciato del Raelismo. Conversazione con l'ex raeliano Jiro Kambe." *Query*, 21: 27–32. www.cicap.org/n/articolo.php?id=276127.

Bigliardi, S. (2015c). "What Would Ron Choose from the Islamic Basket? Notes on Scientology's Construction of Islam." *Temenos*, 51(1): 95–121.

Bigliardi, S. (2016). "New Religious Movements, Technology, and Science: The Conceptualization of the E-Meter in Scientology Teachings." *Zygon*, 51(3): 661–83.

Bigliardi, S. (2017). "Earth as Battlefield and Mission: Knowledge, Technology and Power in L. R. Hubbard's Late Novels." In S. Raine & S. Kent, eds., *Scientology in Popular Culture: Influences and Struggles for Legitimacy*. Santa Barbara, CA: Praeger, pp. 53–79.

Bigliardi, S. (2018). "*Santo Daime* Narratives in Italy: Walter Menozzi, *Stella Azzurra*, and the Conceptualization of Ayahuasca and Science." *Alternative Spirituality and Religion Review*, 9: 190–219.

Bigliardi, S. (2019). "'You Don't Want to Have That Kind of Thought in Your Mind': Li Hongzhi, Aliens, and Science." In J. Lewis & H. Chao, eds., *Enlightened Martyrdom: The Hidden Side of Falun Gong*. Sheffield: Equinox, pp. 162–96.

Bigliardi, S. (2020). "Stella Azzurra." *World Religions and Spirituality Project*. https://wrldrels.org/2020/06/25/stella-azzurra/.

Bigliardi, S. (2021). "Children of Satan (Bambini di Satana)." *World Religions and Spirituality Project*. https://wrldrels.org/2021/10/28/children-of-satan-bambini-di-satana-2/.

Blainey, M. G. (2021). *Christ Returns from the Jungle: Ayahuasca Religion as Mystical Healing*. Albany: State University of New York Press.

Boynton, P. (2013). "Challenging Clitoraid." In S. Jolly, A. Cornwall & K. Hawkins, eds., *Women, Sexuality and the Political Power of Pleasure*. London: Zed Books, pp. 229–50.

Bromley, D. G. (2004). "Perspective: Wither New Religions Studies? Defining and Shaping a New Area of Study." *Nova Religio*, 8(2): 83–97.

Burt, A. (2023). *Hare Krishna in the Twenty-First Century*. Cambridge: Cambridge University Press.

CESNUR. (2021). "I Bambini di Satana." In M. Introvigne & P. L. Zoccatelli, eds., *Le religioni in Italia*. https://cesnur.com/il-satanismo/i-bambini-di-satana/.

Chen, N. N. (2003). *Breathing Spaces: Qigong, Psychiatry, and Healing in China*. New York: Columbia University Press.

Christensen, D. R. (2009). "Sources for the Study of Scientology: Presentations and Reflections." In J. R. Lewis, ed., *Scientology*. New York: Oxford University Press, pp. 411–31.

Church of Scientology International. (2022a). "What Is the E-Meter and How Does It Work?" www.scientology.org/faq/scientology-and-dianetics-auditing/what-is-the-emeter-and-how-does-it-work.html.

Church of Scientology International. (2022b). "Experts Conclude Scientology Is a True World Religion." www.scientologyreligion.org/religious-expertises/.

Citizens' Commission on Human Rights. (2006). *Psychiatry: An Industry of Death*. 108 minutes. www.youtube.com/watch?v=zg0TFkFDtyA&t=1027s.

Clarke, A. C. (2013) [1973]. *Profiles of the Future: An Inquiry into the Limits of the Possible*. New York: Harper & Row.

Clear Wisdom Net. (2001). "What Shanshan Saw in Other Dimensions (II)." April 18/May 2. www.pureinsight.org/node/308.

Clonaid. (2022). Products. www.clonaid.com/page.php?9.

Cole-Turner, R. (2014). "Entheogens, Mysticism, and Neuroscience." *Zygon*, 49(3): 642–51.

Cooper, P. (1971). *The Scandal of Scientology.* Gainesville, FL: Tower. www.cs .cmu.edu/~dst/Library/Shelf/cooper/sos.html.

Corydon, B. & Hubbard Jr., L. R. (1987). *L. Ron Hubbard, Messiah or Madman?* Secaucus, NJ: Lyle Stuart.

Dawson, A. (2013). *Santo Daime: A New World Religion.* London: Bloomsbury.

Dericquebourg, R. (2011). "Legitimizing Belief through the Authority of Science: The Case of the Church of Scientology." In J. R. Lewis and O. Hammer, eds., *Handbook of Religion and the Authority of Science.* Leiden: Brill, pp. 741–62.

Dimitri, M. (undated). *Cos'è la magia.* https://home666.tripod.com/magia .html.

Dimitri, M. (1998). *Il chiodo nel chiodo. Come ti inchiodo il cristiano.* https:// home666.tripod.com/chiodo1.html.

Dimitri, M. (2011). Intervista, Parte 4. MarcoHMCF. www.youtube.com/ watch?v=6pkW1yLNcEo.

Dimitri, M. (2018). Personal communication with author.

Dimitri, M. & Lai, I. (2006). *Dietro lo specchio nero.* Magenta: Iris 4 Edizioni.

Dowell, W. (1999). "Interview with Li Hongzhi." *Time Magazine*, May 10. http://content.time.com/time/world/article/0,8599,2053761,00.html.

Dyrendal, A. (2011). "'Oh No, It Isn't.' Sceptics and the Rhetorical Use of Science in Religion." In J. R. Lewis and O. Hammer, eds., *Handbook of Religion and the Authority of Science.* Leiden: Brill, pp. 879–900.

Farley, H. (2011). "Falun Gong and Science: Origins, Pseudoscience and China's Scientific Establishment." In J. R. Lewis & O. Hammer, eds., *Handbook of Religion and the Authority of Science.* Leiden: Brill, pp. 141–63.

Farley, H. (2014). "Falun Gong: A Narrative of Pending Apocalypse, Shape-Shifting Aliens and Relentless Persecution." In J. R. Lewis & J. A. Petersen, eds., *Controversial New Religions*, 2nd ed., New York: Oxford University Press, pp. 241–56.

Glossary of Scientology & Dianetics Terms (2000–2015). www.whatisscientol ogy.org/html/Part14/Chp50/pg1021.html.

Grünschloß, A. (2009). "Scientology: A 'New Age' Religion?" In J. R. Lewis, ed., *Scientology.* New York: Oxford University Press, pp. 225–43.

Hammer, O. (2004) [2001]. *Claiming Knowledge: Strategies of Epistemology from Theosophy to the New Age.* Leiden: Brill.

Hanegraaff, W. J. (1998). *New Age Religion and Western Culture. Esotericism in the Mirror of Secular Thought.* Albany: State University of New York Press.

Helland, C. (2007). "The Raëlian Creation Myth and the Art of Cloning: Reality or Rhetoric?" In D. G. Tumminia, ed., *Alien Worlds: Social and Religious*

Dimensions of the UFO Phenomenon. Syracuse: Syracuse University Press, pp. 275–99.

Hubbard, L. R. (1950a). "Dianetics: The Evolution of a Science." *Astounding Science Fiction*, 45: 43–87.

Hubbard, L. R. (1950b). *Dianetics: The Modern Science of Mental Health.* New York: Hermitage House.

Hubbard, L. R. (1957). *All About Radiation.* London: The Hubbard Association of Scientologists International.

Hubbard, L. R. (1961). "Personal Integrity." *Ability,* 125. www.scientology.org/what-is-scientology/basic-principles-of-scientology/personal-integrity.html.

Hubbard, L. R. (1965). "Keeping Scientology Working Series 1." Hubbard Communications Office Policy Letter of February 7.

Hubbard, L. R. (1983) [1966]. *The Book Introducing the E-Meter.* Copenhagen: New Era Publications International.

Hubbard, L. R. (1989) [1982]. *Understanding the E-Meter.* Copenhagen: New Era Publications International.

Hubbard, L. R. (2005) [1982]. *Battlefield Earth: A Saga of the Year 3000.* Los Angeles: Galaxy Press.

Hubbard, L. R. (2006) [1961]. *E-Meter Essentials.* Copenhagen: New Era Publications International.

Hubbard, L. R. (2007a) [1952]. "Indoctrination in the Use of the E-Meter." Lecture and auditing demonstration, March 8. Transcript in *Scientology: Milestone One.* Los Angeles: Golden Era Productions, pp. 186–238.

Hubbard, L. R. (2007b) [1952]. *Scientology: A History of Man. A List and Description of the Principal Incidents to be Found in a Human Being.* Copenhagen: New Era Publications International.

Hummel, L. (2014). "By Its Fruits? Mystical and Visionary States of Consciousness Occasioned by Entheogens." *Zygon* 49(3): 685–95.

Introvigne, M. (2010). *I satanisti. Storia, riti e miti del satanismo.* Milano: Sugarco Edizioni.

Introvigne, M. (2017). "Scientology: Genesis, Exodus, and Numbers – Fake News about Scientology Statistics." *CESNUR.* www.cesnur.org/2017/scientology_numbers.htm.

Jacobsen, J. (2009). "The E-Meter Experts." *Infinite Complacency.* http://infinitecomplacency.blogspot.com/2009/07/13-e-meter-experts_24.html.

Kambe, J. (2012). "Raëlism vs. Science: THE CLONE DILEMMA." *Raëlian "Truth."* https://raelian-truth.blogspot.com/2012/01/raelism-vs-science-clone-dilemma.html.

Kuhn, T. (1962). *The Structure of Scientific Revolutions.* Chicago: University of Chicago Press.

Lerma, A. (1999). "The E-Meter Papers." *lermanet.com.* www.lermanet.com/e-metershort.htm.

Lewis, J. R. (2003). *Legitimating New Religions.* New Brunswick, NJ: Rutgers University Press.

Lewis, J. R. (2011). "How Religions Appeal to the Authority of Science." In J. R. Lewis and O. Hammer, eds., *Handbook of Religion and the Authority of Science.* Leiden: Brill, pp. 23–40.

Lewis, J. R. & Hammer, O. eds. (2011). *Handbook of Religion and the Authority of Science.* Leiden: Brill.

Li, H. (1996). *Zhuan Falun*, Volume II. https://falundafa.org/eng/eng/html/zfl2/zfl2.htm.

Li, H. (1997). "Fa Teaching Given in San Francisco" [April 6]. In Hongzhi Li, (2014), *Falun Buddha Fa. Fa Teachings in the United States*, https://en.falundafa.org/eng/pdf/mgjf.pdf; pp. 22–35.

Li, H. (1998a). Teaching the Fa at the Conference in Europe [Frankfurt, May 30–31]. www.falundafa.org/book/eng/europe1998a.htm.

Li, H. (1998b). Teachings at the Conference in Singapore [August 22–23]. https://en.falundafa.org/eng/lectures/19980822L.html.

Li, H. (1998c). Teaching the Fa at the Conference in Switzerland [Geneva, September 4–5]. www.falundafa.org/book/eng/switzerland1998.htm.

Li, H. (1999). Teachings at the Conference in the Western U.S. [Los Angeles, February 21–22]. http://en.falundafa.org/eng/lectures/19990221L.html.

Li, H. (2001). Teaching the Fa at the 2001 Canada Fa Conference [Ottawa, May 19]. https://falundafa.org/eng/eng/pdf/daohang.pdf.; pp. 15–18.

Li, H. (2018). *Zhuan Falun.* https://falundafa.org/eng/eng/pdf/ZFL2014.pdf.

Lloyd-Roberts, S. (2014). "FGM, Clitoraid and the Pleasure Hospital: US Sect the Raëlians' Quest to 'Restore' Women Scarred by Female Genital Mutilation in Burkina Faso." *The Independent*, March 16. www.independent.co.uk/news/world/africa/fgm-clitoraid-and-the-pleasure-hospital-us-sect-the-ra-lians-quest-to-restore-women-scarred-by-9195795.html.

Machado, C. (2010). "Science, Fiction, and Religion: About Raël and Raëlian Possible Worlds." In S. Aupers and D. Houtman, eds., *Religions of Modernity: Relocating the Sacred to the Self and the Digital.* Leiden: Brill, pp. 187–204.

McKenna, T. (1993). *True Hallucinations: Being an Account of the Author's Extraordinary Adventures in the Devil's Paradise.* San Francisco, CA: HarperSanFrancisco.

Melton, J. G. (2004). "Perspective: Toward a Definition of 'New Religion'." *Nova Religio*, 8(1): 73–87.

Menozzi, W. (2013) [2007]. *Ayahuasca: La Liana degli Spiriti—Il sacramento magico-religioso dello sciamanismo amazzonico.* Rome: Edizioni Spazio Interiore.

Menozzi, W. (2016). Personal communication with author.

Menozzi, W. (2020). Personal communication with author.

Meyer, M. (2013). "Currents, Fluids, and Forces: The Contribution of Esotericist Philosophy to the Development of Brazil's Ayahuasca Religions." Paper presented at the Psychedelic Science 2013 Conference. Oakland, CA, April 18–23.

Mickler, M. (2023). *The Unification Church Movement.* Cambridge: Cambridge University Press.

Miller, R. (1987). *Bare-Faced Messiah: The True Story of L. Ron Hubbard.* London: M. Joseph.

Ortega, T. (2014). "Jon Takes Apart the Scientology E-Meter." *The Underground Bunker.* https://tonyortega.org/2014/02/01/jon-atack-takes-apart-the-scientology-emeter/.

Ownby, D. (2008). *Falun Gong and the Future of China.* New York: Oxford University Press.

Palmer, D. A. (2007). *Qigong Fever: Body, Science and Utopia in China.* New York: Columbia University Press.

Palmer, S. J. (2003). "From Healing to Protest: Conversion Patterns among the Practitioners of Falun Gong." *Nova Religio*, 6(2): 348–64.

Palmer, S. J. (2004). *Aliens Adored: Raël's UFO Religion.* New Brunswick, NJ: Rutgers University Press.

Palmer, S. J. & Ownby, D. (2000). "Field Notes: Falun Dafa Practitioners: A Preliminary Research Report." *Nova Religio*, 4(1): 133–37.

Paolinelli, P. (2007). "Esoterismo, sicurezza e comunicazione. Il caso dei Bambini di Satana." *La critica sociologica*, 161: 38–85.

Partridge, C. (2004). "Alternative Spiritualities, New Religions, and the Reenchantment of the West." In J. R. Lewis, ed., *New Religious Movements.* New York: Oxford University Press, pp. 39–67.

Penny, B. (2003). "The Life and Times of Li Hongzhi: Falun Gong and Religious Biography." *The China Quarterly*, 175: 643–71.

Penny, B. (2012). *The Religion of Falun Gong.* Chicago: University of Chicago Press.

Peters, T. (2018). "Science and Religion: Ten Models of War, Truce, and Partnership." *Theology and Science*, 16(1): 11–53.

Petersen, J. A. (2011). "'We Demand Bedrock Knowledge': Modern Satanism Between Secularized Esotericism and 'Esotericized' Secularism." In

J. R. Lewis & O. Hammer, eds., *Handbook of Religion and the Authority of Science*. Leiden: Brill, pp. 67–114.

Pigliucci, M. & Boudry, M. (2013). *Philosophy of Pseudoscience: Reconsidering the Demarcation Problem*. Chicago: University of Chicago Press.

Richards, W. A. (2015). *Sacred Knowledge: Psychedelics and Religious Experience*. New York: Columbia University Press.

Richter, J. (2012). "Traces of the Gods: Ancient Astronauts as a Vision of Our Future." *Numen*, 59(2/3): 222–48.

Robbins, T. (2004). "Perspective. New Religions and Alternative Religions." *Nova Religio*, 8(3): 104–11.

Rothstein, M. (2008). "Science and Religion in the New Religions." In J. R. Lewis, ed., *The Oxford Handbook of New Religious Movements*. New York: Oxford University Press, pp. 99–118.

Sacco, L. (2011). "Is Falun Gong a Sect or a Religious Movement? A Comparative Approach." *Historia Religionum*, 3: 65–76.

Santucci, J. A. (2008). "The Notion of Race in Theosophy." *Nova Religio*, 11 (3): 37–63.

Schafmeister, C. (undated). "Biophysics and the E-Meter." www.cs.cmu.edu/~dst/ Secrets/E-Meter/biophysics.html.

Scientology Spiritual Technology. (2014). Super Bowl Advertisement. 1.03 minutes. www.youtube.com/watch?v=QavEOfgeOi4.

Sentes, B. & Palmer, S. J. (2000). "Presumed Immanent: The Raëlians, UFO Religions, and the Postmodern Condition." *Nova Religio*, 4(1): 86–105.

Shamir, Y. (2020). *The Prophet and the Space Aliens*. Yoav Shamir Films. 86 minutes.

Stenmark, M. (2004). *How to Relate Science and Religion: A Multidimensional Model*. Grand Rapids, MI: William B. Eerdmans.

Stoczkowski, W. (1999). *Des hommes, des dieux, et des extraterrestres. Ethnologie d'une croyance moderne*. Paris: Flammarion.

Strickland, E. (2008). "Raëlians Rocket from Clones to Clitorises." *Wired*, February 19. https://web.archive.org/web/20100213070438/http://www .wired.com/science/discoveries/news/2008/02/hospital.

Thomas, A. (2021). *Free Zone Scientology: Contesting the Boundaries of a New Religion*. London: Bloomsbury.

Urban, H. B. (2011). *The Church of Scientology: A History of a New Religion*. Princeton, NJ: Princeton University Press.

USA Today. (2003). "With Friends Like These, Monsanto Needs no Enemies." https://usatoday30.usatoday.com/tech/news/techpolicy/2003-08-06-raelians-biotech_x.htm.

Von Stuckrad, K. (2015). *The Scientification of Religion: An Historical Study of Discursive Change 1800–2000*. Berlin: Walter de Gruyter.

Vorilhon, C. [Raël] (1974). *Le livre qui dit la vérité. J'ai rencontré un extraterrestre*. Clermont-Ferrand: L'Edition du Message.

Vorilhon, C. [Raël] (1977a). *Les extra-terrestres m'ont emmené sur leur planète. Le 2ème message qu'ils m'ont donné*. Clermont-Ferrand: L'Edition du Message.

Vorilhon, C. [Raël] (1977b). *Geniocracy: Government of the People, for the People, by the Geniuses*. Translated by Marcus Wenner & Eva Ponty (2008). N.p.: Nova Distribution.

Vorilhon, C. [Raël] (2001). *Yes to Human Cloning: Eternal Life Thanks to Science*. Translated by Marcus Wenner. Vaduz, Liechtenstein: The Raëlian Foundation.

Wallis, R. (1984). *The Elementary Forms of the New Religious Life*. London: Routledge & Kegan Paul.

Westbrook, D. A. (2016). Personal communication with author.

Westbrook, D. A. (2017). "'The Enemy of My Enemy is My Friend': Thomas Szasz, the Citizens Commission on Human Rights, and Scientology's Anti-Psychiatric Theology." *Nova Religio*, 20(4): 37–61.

Westbrook, D. A. (2019). *Among the Scientologists. History, Theology, and Praxis*. New York: Oxford University Press.

Westbrook, D. A. (2022a). *L. Ron Hubbard and Scientology Studies*. Cambridge: Cambridge University Press.

Westbrook, D. A. (2022b). Personal communication with author.

Zeller, B. E. (2010). *Prophets and Protons: New Religious Movements and Science in Late Twentieth-Century America*. New York: New York University Press.

Zeller, B. E. (2011). "New Religious Movements and Science." *Nova Religio*, 14(4): 4–10.

Zeller, B. E. (2014). *Heaven's Gate: America's UFO Religion*. New York: New York University Press.

Acknowledgments

To the best of my memory, I was first exposed to scholarly work on NRMs and science through Josef Schovanec's talk "More Scientific than Scientists. When Extreme Scientific Narratives Become a PR Strategy of New Religions," on March 2, 2012, at the conference *Religions, Science and Technology in Cultural Contexts: Dynamics of Change* in Trondheim at the Norwegian University of Science and Technology. However, I began systematic interaction with NRM specialists in June 2014 at the International Conference in Waco, Texas, organized at Baylor University by CESNUR (Centro Studi sulle Nuove Religioni, Turin), the International Society for the Study of New Religions, and the Baylor Institute for Studies of Religion. I made a presentation on Islamic creationism: originally trained in the philosophy of science, I had transitioned to the study of Islam and contemporary science. While attending exciting presentations, I realized that several typologies for the study of religion and science, modeled on major monotheisms, could be extended to the study of less-known and widespread, but to me even more intriguing, NRMs. The open-minded, welcoming attitude of colleagues trained in fields different from mine was decisive to have me step into the field. Over the following years, I had enlightening conversations with multiple scholars to whom I am very thankful, including those who provided me with information, material, and feedback for this Element. I can mention here, with gratitude, Eileen Barker, Debbora Battaglia, Marc Blainey, Nancy N. Chen, Adam J. Chin, Andrew Dawson, Régis Dericquebourg, Bernard Doherty, Helen Farley, Nidhal Guessoum, Olav Hammer, Massimo Introvigne, Stephen Kent, Susan J. Palmer, Susan Raine, Mikael Rothstein, Leonardo Sacco, Mikael Stenmark, Kocku von Stuckrad, Donald A. Westbrook, Gereon Wolters, Benjamin E. Zeller, and PierLuigi Zoccatelli.

I am also thankful to all the practitioners who patiently helped me familiarize with their respective movements and beliefs.

I am deeply indebted to the late Professor James Lewis, this Element's series Founding Editor, for thinking of me as a suitable author for this Element. I extend my gratitude to Professor Rebecca Moore, Series Editor, for her generosity and patience.

My university graces its instructors, on a biennial basis, with one nonteaching summer. While drawing upon research (including armchair investigations and fieldwork), scholarly interactions, and publications occurring since 2014, this Element was written between late May and late August 2022. I am thankful to Professor Chris Taylor, the Vice President for Academic Affairs and interim

Dean of the School of Humanities and Social Sciences at Al Akhawayn University in Ifrane, for the opportunity to spend the period in Italy.

I also owe a big debt of gratitude to my parents, Adelmo and Regina, for arranging everything so as to grant me a peaceful and productive summer stay at our family home.

Cambridge Elements $\equiv$

New Religious Movements

Founding Editor

†James R. Lewis

Wuhan University

The late James R. Lewis was Professor of Philosophy at Wuhan University, China. He served as the editor or co-editor for four book series, was the general editor for the *Alternative Spirituality and Religion Review*, and the associate editor for the *Journal of Religion and Violence*. His publications include *The Cambridge Companion to Religion and Terrorism* (Cambridge University Press 2017) and *Falun Gong: Spiritual Warfare and Martyrdom* (Cambridge University Press 2018).

Series Editor

Rebecca Moore

San Diego State University

Rebecca Moore is Emerita Professor of Religious Studies at San Diego State University. She has written and edited numerous books and articles on Peoples Temple and the Jonestown tragedy. She has served as co-general editor or reviews editor of *Nova Religio* since 2000. Publications include *Beyond Brainwashing: Perspectives on Cult Violence* (Cambridge University Press 2018) and *Peoples Temple and Jonestown in the Twenty-First Century* (Cambridge University Press 2022).

About the Series

Elements in New Religious Movements go beyond cult stereotypes and popular prejudices to present new religions and their adherents in a scholarly and engaging manner. Case studies of individual groups, such as Transcendental Meditation and Scientology, provide in-depth consideration of some of the most well known, and controversial, groups. Thematic examinations of women, children, science, technology, and other topics focus on specific issues unique to these groups. Historical analyses locate new religions in specific religious, social, political, and cultural contexts.

These examinations demonstrate why some groups exist in tension with the wider society and why others live peaceably in the mainstream. The series highlights the differences, as well as the similarities, within this great variety of religious expressions. To discuss contributing to this series please contact Professor Moore, remoore@sdsu.edu.

Cambridge Elements ≡

New Religious Movements

Printed in the United States
by Baker & Taylor Publisher Services